Time & Stress Management
for ROOKIES

Titles in the *for* ROOKIES series

Dealing with Difficult People for Rookies by Frances Kay
Emotional Intelligence for Rookies by Andrea Bacon & Ali Dawson
Generation Y for Rookies by Sally Bibb
Job Hunting for Rookies by Rob Yeung
Low-Budget Marketing for Rookies by Karen McCreadie
Negotiation Skills for Rookies by Patrick Forsyth
NLP for Rookies by Rebecca Mallery & Katherine Russell
Social Networking for Rookies by Tina Bettison
Time & Stress Management for Rookies by Frances Kay

About the author

With many years' work experience, covering politics, diplomatic service and law, **Frances Kay** has a wide range of contacts and works with organizations in the field of research and corporate development. Frances coaches, trains and advises on all aspects of personal and career development and professional relationship building. An experienced author, she has had twenty business books published, including *New Kid on the Block* and *Hello, I Must Be Going: the wallflower's guide to networking*, both published by Marshall Cavendish.

Time & Stress Management
for ROOKIES

LID

mc Marshall Cavendish
Business

Copyright © 2009 LID Editorial Empresarial and Marshall Cavendish Limited

First published in 2009 by

Marshall Cavendish Limited
Fifth Floor
32–38 Saffron Hill
London EC1N 8FH
United Kingdom
T: +44 (0)20 7421 8120
F: +44 (0)20 7421 8121
sales@marshallcavendish.co.uk
www.marshallcavendish.co.uk

A member of BPR
businesspublishersroundtable.com

Marshall Cavendish is a trademark of Times Publishing Limited

Other Marshall Cavendish offices: Marshall Cavendish International (Asia) Private Limited, 1 New Industrial Road, Singapore 536196 • Marshall Cavendish Corporation. 99 White Plains Road, Tarrytown NY 10591–9001, USA • Marshall Cavendish International (Thailand) Co Ltd. 253 Asoke, 12th Floor, Sukhumvit 21 Road, Klongtoey Nua, Wattana, Bangkok 10110, Thailand • Marshall Cavendish (Malaysia) Sdn Bhd, Times Subang, Lot 46, Subang Hi-Tech Industrial Park, Batu Tiga, 40000 Shah Alam, Selangor Darul Ehsan, Malaysia

All rights reserved

No part of this publication may be reproduced, stored in a retrieval system or transmitted, in any form or by any means, electronic, mechanical, photocopying, recording or otherwise, without the prior permission of the copyright owner. Requests for permission should be addressed to the publisher.

The author and publisher have used their best efforts in preparing this book and disclaim liability arising directly and indirectly from the use and application of this book.

All reasonable efforts have been made to obtain necessary copyright permissions. Any omissions or errors are unintentional and will, if brought to the attention of the publisher, be corrected in future printings.

A CIP record for this book is available from the British Library

ISBN 978-0-462-09955-2

Illustrations by Nuria Aparicio and Joan Guardiet

Printed and bound in Great Britain by
TJ International Limited, Padstow, Cornwall

Contents

	Introduction	7
1.	Time management: what is it?	11
2.	Stress management: how it fits in	27
3.	Identifying your personal style	43
4.	Time and stress management: first steps	59
5.	Formulating an action plan	73
6.	Dealing with interruptions	87
7.	Technology and time management	101
8.	Paper: one of the greatest time wasters	113
9.	People are time-consuming too	125
10.	Motivation for keeping up the good work	139
	Appendix: Attitude training	151
	Index	155

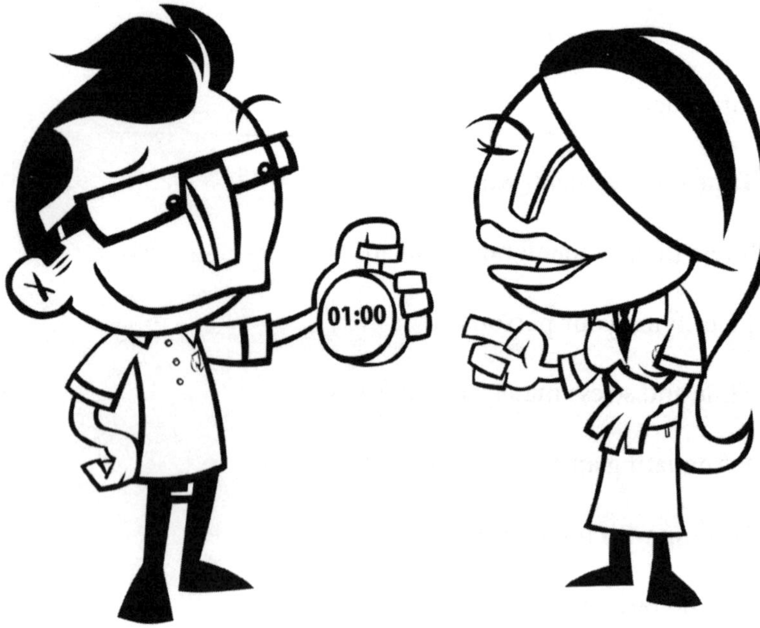
01:00

Introduction

Whoever you are, whatever you do, you have things you want to achieve. To get things done it helps to be organized. In other words, those who are best prepared are more likely to accomplish things than those who aren't. If you can't manage your time, you'll find that the hours pass, no matter what. And if there's nothing to show for it, this can be upsetting. Why are people so obsessed about how they spend their time? When days fly by without much being achieved, is that such a problem? And why do people worry so much about it?

Do you find you are often apologizing for missed deadlines and broken promises, and not delivering what you've agreed? There's sometimes even a degree of pride in someone's voice when they talk about being overworked and under pressure. Are they afraid that if other people thought they simply had "enough" to do, rather than "too much", they might be considered less important?

There's a lot written about how overwhelming life is: indeed there is often a lot to do. Sometimes you just don't have enough time or resources for the task in hand. But that's only a problem if you don't have strategies and tactics for dealing with such issues. The purpose of this book is to provide you with practical ideas and easy-to-follow methods that you can put into practice immediately. It will equip you with the skills for keeping your head (when all about you may be losing theirs). If you can do this, not only will your time management be good, but your personal effectiveness will improve and your confidence increase. That will do a lot to keep the stress levels from red-lining.

In the 21st century it's perhaps fashionable to be time poor. Also, in some people's minds being "stressed" is part of today's business culture. If you're not "overworking", maybe you're not working hard enough. Certainly having so much choice means that life can be full of challenges. For example, there is a multitude of ways to communicate with people today – face to face, over the phone, by email, text message, letter or fax. Which is the most appropriate? It wasn't all that long ago that if something was urgent, you went to see someone about it. If it was less urgent, you wrote them a letter. If it wasn't all that important you probably did nothing about it. And who knows, perhaps it didn't matter all that much.

With IT changing and progressing faster than ever, the demand for increased productivity is always there. Technology can (and does) make everything happen faster – when it's going well it is very good. But if it goes wrong, it goes wrong a lot faster too. Mistakes reach epic proportions in a matter of seconds. This leads to people feeling more exhausted and stressed. The expectation of "instant gratification" also adds to the stress factor. Because you're expected to be available and "on call" 24/7/365, it's not surprising you feel worn out – if not all the time, at least on a fairly frequent basis.

This book is designed to help those who want to combat stress and take control of work situations. You may find that rather than getting more out of your day, and speeding up and doing things faster, it's more helpful if you spend time thinking about what you really ought to be doing. This could mean that you do less (of the wrong sort of things) so that you have more time to work out how to do the right things. Less can sometimes mean more. I hope that makes you feel better.

By the time you've finished this book you should feel that you're no longer fire fighting, lurching from problem to crisis. There are methods, tools, techniques and practical advice in here – even a maintenance plan for good habits. You will feel more relaxed because you're less stressed. So then you can enjoy the time that you have saved.

You won't be a Rookie any more – you'll have the means of dealing with pressure, in a healthier way. You'll be equipped to handle the elements of surprise that can dramatically impact on your work time. If you want to improve your performance, increase your efficiency, work more effectively and achieve greater output in a smoother manner – this is the book for you to read. Now surely you can find time to do that?

Time management is something most people think they understand. It actually sounds quite simple, but there is a lot more to it than at first appears. What is good time management to one person may be completely the opposite to another. This chapter sets out a general definition of time management and a discussion about what it means to different people. It also gives basic guidance on the various ways to tackle it.

CHAPTER 1

Time management: what is it?

The purpose of this general advice is to introduce the various aspects of time management. It should help you identify what time management means to you. Once you understand the principles, you will be able to work out what methods of dealing with time management will be most useful to you. Perhaps you will have identified areas of particular concern? The aim, at the end of the book, is for you to have a number of practical time management solutions easily accessible when you need them. This should keep your confidence, productivity and effectiveness at a high level.

Understanding time management

Time is a valuable resource. Why? Because you can't buy it, keep it or stop it in its tracks. Every minute that passes has gone, forever. You can't recover it, rewind it or recycle it. So it pays to treat time with respect and try to get the best result out of every precious moment. If you want to maximize its potential, you need to manage your actions well.

> **Rookie Buster**
>
> Being good at managing your time means being organized, efficient and using your time wisely.

No one can remember everything, however good a memory they have. Being good at managing your time means being organized, efficient and using your time wisely. One thing that's very useful is spending a bit of time thinking about your priorities, working out what needs to be done by when. This is not time wasted. In fact it's a wise investment of an hour or so.

Most people from time to time experience the problem of not knowing how to get everything done in the time available. This is quite normal. It doesn't mean that you are bad at managing your time. However, if this sort of problem seems to be constant in your life to one degree or another, you do have a time management dilemma. There are times for everyone when things seem to conspire to prevent work going ahead as planned. But if you're about to confess to living in a state of near-permanent chaos, you need to take action.

You probably do have too much to do, and too little time in which to do it. Perhaps while coping with the urgent tasks you never get around to the really important ones. Is your desk piled high with untidy sheaves of paper? Are you bombarded with interruptions on a daily basis and impossible deadlines foisted on you?

> **Rookie Buster**
>
> The effect of getting to grips with your time management has several positive (immediate) benefits. It improves your efficiency, effectiveness and productivity. And it can influence how you are perceived by others in your workplace.

Time management should be seen alongside self management. To be a good time manager demands discipline, but discipline reinforced by good habits. The effect of getting to grips with your time management has several positive (immediate) benefits. It improves your efficiency, effectiveness and productivity. And it can influence how you are perceived by others in your workplace.

It can also shift the pressure that goes with the job so that you are not suffering from negative stress. (There's more about stress in the next chapter.) Working effectively certainly helps, because being effective is about getting the right things done. But you have to keep an eye on what's ahead of you – this requires some planning skills too.

Many people think they are good at managing their time because they are doing things in an efficient way. But if you aren't doing the right things, you've fallen into the common trap of confusing efficiency with effectiveness. Effective time management means knowing what's important and focusing on those items rather than the insignificant ones. It doesn't matter how well you do routine or unimportant tasks if they are time wasting activities.

Rookie Buster

Effective time management means knowing what's important and focusing on those items rather than the insignificant ones.

Making it work

To be successful, you need to develop skills and habits which, when used correctly, work positively for you. These skills aren't only necessary for doing your job successfully, they are also essential if you want to be seen as competent and capable.

First, it helps to be organized. This applies both at work and at home. If you are being led by events rather than being in control, it is quite likely that this impacts on your leisure time too. Every constructive habit you learn will help. In other words, there's good news. It gets easier as you go along. Good time management habits help ensure a well-organized approach to the way you plan and carry out your work. Bad habits, as the saying goes, are like beds. They are easy to get into but difficult to get out of.

> **Rookie Buster**
>
> Making time management work for you relies on two key factors: how you plan your time and how you implement the detail of what you've planned.

There is nothing worse than getting to the end of the day feeling you've achieved little or nothing. Making time management work for you relies on two key factors: how you plan your time, and how you implement the detail of what you've planned. Some of the skills you will be learning later on are: how to plan; self-assessment; making a plan; and setting goals.

Here's a brief explanation of them to give you an idea of what they are.

Planning

This is a prerequisite to all action. Whatever the task you have to do, you should research, investigate and analyse it. If it's complex, test how you will carry it out, consult with others if there is no clear answer, keep communicating, and then make your decision as to how you will do it. One tip about planning is to make sure you start the day well. The way you deal with the first hour of the day can dictate how you'll cope with the rest of it. If you can make that first hour productive (even if you are compiling your To Do list – see later) you will set a good trend. By focusing on what you want to achieve and allowing your mind to formulate a plan as to how you'll get there, you will be well on the way to a positive result.

Self-assessment

If you want to improve something, you need to know how good or bad it is at the moment. Without a benchmark against which progress can be measured, how can you effect any change? You may want to work out which areas are the ones that need the greatest improvement. Perhaps you spend hours on the phone, or sit in endless unnecessary meetings? What is the main drain on your time? Is it too much paperwork, or just a messy desk? You can't begin to answer such questions without knowing (honestly) what your work practices are really like. In other words, exactly where does your time go?

Making a plan

You can't make much real progress in time management without a written plan. This should ideally be reviewed and updated regularly. It could be a daily check, showing accurately and completely the work plan for the immediate future. Some things are quite easy to include – regular commitments of anticipated activities for the months ahead. But some are less clear because they cannot be forecast much in advance, if at all. (You don't know when fuel prices are likely to increase or when interest rates are going to change because these things are beyond your control.) What you are aiming to do is create a time management discipline. The information would include: what you do, what you delegate (if anything), what you delay, what you ignore, and the order in which you tackle things.

Setting goals

Before you can work effectively you need to work out what is important. This may sound simple and obvious, but don't underestimate how much it influences your effectiveness. If you can work out which goals are worth the effort and which are the key issues, you will be able to identify the tasks which have a dramatic effect on your time management. Again, some things will be clear, others less so. The best time managers (and this is surely what you are going to become) concentrate time and energy on priorities. What will make you an outstanding time manager is your ability to make prompt and firm decisions about what the priorities are. You don't want to be one of those who spends hours thinking about what should come first, only to review the decision again and again and then change your mind. Of course circumstances can change, but all that is required here is an ongoing review of tasks and goals.

Now let's have a look at a few time management myths:

Efficiency and effectiveness mean the same thing

Wrong! Being efficient is doing something quickly and properly even if it is a fairly mindless routine task. But in itself it isn't good time management. Effectiveness is all about doing the right things, recognizing a priority task when you see one. If you do the right things at the right time, you'll end up achieving your objectives. And that will mean you've also managed your time well.

If you want a job done properly, do it yourself

No, not necessarily. One of the core principles of time management is having the ability and willingness to delegate. If you can't, or won't, delegate, your time management will be poor and your productivity low. No one can (nor should they) do everything, however brilliant they are. Sometimes people fail to delegate because they don't know how to (more on this later). But if you spend your time doing things that ought to be done by someone else, you won't be able to focus on what you really should be doing. Once you can do that, you will notice a huge improvement in what you achieve. The ability and willingness to delegate is paramount if you want to use your time correctly. The opposite – unwillingness or inability to delegate properly – is one of the main reasons for poor output.

A task must always be performed in the same way

Why? Everyone is familiar with the saying: "If you do what you've always done, you'll get what you've always got." At work you may see someone do something in a way you find most peculiar. When you ask them why, they will probably tell you they've always done it like that. It is amazing how much time is wasted doing things in the same way, even when it doesn't work. Maybe the reason people are resistant to change is fear of the unknown and lack of time to consider things properly. One of the rules of time management is to spend time thinking about things before you do them. Don't rush headlong into something if, after a few moments' reflection, you could improve the situation hugely by doing things differently. The ability to be flexible, and not get stuck in a rut, is a great help towards good time management. Think outside the box – not inside it.

There's no time for time management

If you're under that much pressure, you really can't be managing your time at all well. Stop and think – do some planning. There's no room for headless chickens around here. A good time manager needs to spend some time each day making plans and thinking carefully. You may not look busy while you're doing it (thinking, that is), but it is a common error to confuse "busyness" with "output". If you take the time to plan your daily schedule and work out what really need to be accomplished, you'll have far less pressure on your time.

If you're creative you can't be a good time manager

Some creative people are very proud of the fact that they can't manage time. They wear it as a badge of honour – some don't wear watches to prove their point. They think inspiration and effectiveness are incompatible. But if you know what good time management techniques are, you can use them as creatively as you wish. It may be a simple matter of getting up half an hour earlier to avoid the rush hour into work. It doesn't sound all that inspirational, but it could have an immensely beneficial effect on your day. It is amazing sometimes the result you get from changing one thing, just a little. The knock-on effect can be far greater than you would have thought. There are lots of small techniques you will learn that will make an enormous difference to your time management and output. You are limited only by your own energy and ability. But remember, it's extremely difficult to be imaginative when there's a panic on and you're managing a crisis.

Sorting yourself out

Do you spend a part of each day thinking and planning? Many people think they do, and would answer Yes. But perhaps, if you're absolutely honest, you don't spend much time thinking about what you do and how long it takes you to do it. Sometimes all it takes is a bit of planning – what you need to do, and what you want to achieve.

After all, there's little point in making plans before you know the full facts and implications. You are more likely to come up with the best ideas and strategies if you allow a little flexibility in your thinking. Good time management techniques shouldn't be too rigid.

> **Rookie Buster**
>
> Good time management techniques shouldn't be too rigid.

Lots of people have problems with time management. Don't think for one moment that you are on your own. Here are some of the reasons that people suffer from a lack of time control.

1. **Unable to plan**

    Some people have an inability to plan. As you've already learned, you need to be organized in order to manage your time well. Planning and organizational tips are detailed further on, so you can overcome chaos and bring discipline and order into your life.

2. **Interruptions occur**

    If you aren't able to avoid interruptions (whether from people or machines) you will find time management extremely difficult. You will learn to deal with them effectively and professionally so that your day is not left open to chance.

3. **Procrastination**

    Perhaps the biggest single cause of time management failure is people putting off doing things. Maybe a task is too big or too daunting, or you simply dislike the job and would do anything to avoid it. Or could it be fear of failure?

Ways to overcome delaying tactics are essential skills in your time management tool kit.

4. **Crisis management**
   From time to time, crises will occur. They cannot all be prevented. But if you are unable to manage your time, a crisis could become a catastrophe. This could be simply because there are no organizational procedures to support you.

5. **Decision making**
   Being able to take decisions and make them work is one way of getting to grips with time management issues. The reasons why people fail to make decisions could be because they don't know how to, or because they don't know what makes the difference between a good decision and a bad one.

6. **Being perfect**
   Good time management doesn't mean doing everything so well that it cannot be improved upon. In fact, where time management is concerned it could be that "good enough" is often sufficient. The Pareto Principle (also known as the 80/20 Rule) states that 20 per cent of effort produces 80 per cent of results – and that 80 per cent is often good enough. Applying this is one of the most useful time management skills.

We'll look at all these topics in greater detail one by one. You'll have a complete guide to improving your organizational skills, your work processes and your complete time management.

So before moving on to operational tactics, let's recap on the main issues.

However you look at it, time management and the bottom line are closely connected. Poor time management is costly – to you, to your employer, to your company. You can't afford *not* to do it well. From an employer's viewpoint it is easily quantifiable in terms of wages or salaries. But these costs are perhaps the least of the problem. Some of the other cost factors involved in poor time management are:

- Loss of control.
- Stress.
- Underachievement.
- Waste of resources.
- Opportunities lost.
- Poor communication.
- Lack of motivation.
- Low morale.
- Inability to respond to change.

> **Rookie Buster**
>
> Poor time management is costly – to you, to your employer, to your company. You can't afford NOT to do it well.

The list could be much longer than this. Managing time creates opportunities so you do the things you should be doing. By planning and managing your time correctly you will improve your performance and achieve the outcome you want. People who can't (or won't) manage their time are likely to be inefficient and ineffective. Tasks take longer, mistakes occur, things get lost or left out.

> **Rookie Buster**
>
> Managing time creates opportunities so you do the things you should be doing. By planning and managing your time correctly you will improve your performance and achieve the outcome you want.

In the following chapters you will learn – amongst other things – about yourself, how to plan, prioritize and write lists. But you will also form good time management habits, create systems that work smoothly (for you) and learn strategies for coping with the unexpected.

Coach's notes

This chapter has explained a bit about time management, why it's important and how you should go about learning some time management skills.

To get to grips with the principles of time management, remember:

- It's not the hours you put in, it's what you put into the hours.
- Time management isn't just about time, it's about tasks too.
- Effective time management is a real asset to anyone's productivity.
- It helps you to stay in control, handling the elements of surprise that can occur.
- If you can cope with interruptions, problems and crises, you won't be firefighting.
- Time management prevents procrastination which causes many problems.
- Being organized is essential. Prepare, plan and focus in order to achieve more.
- The inability to say "No" plays havoc with controlling time.
- Effective time managers aim to work smarter rather than harder or longer hours.
- The quickest way to do many things is to do one of them at a time.

Go for it! Time management is not only about time, it's about tasks. If you learn to manage your time well, you will achieve more and get good results from your actions. To be successful you need to develop skills and habits which, when used correctly, work positively to spur you on. These skills not only help you to do your job well, they allow you to be seen as a capable and competent person.

It helps if you're organized too. Luckily the techniques of good time management are many and varied. There is something to suit everyone. Once you understand the principles you will be able to adapt the rules and apply them to your own individual circumstances. A tailored approach always works best. Every constructive habit you develop will enhance your time management and help you avoid excessive stress.

Notes

Leaving time management aside for the moment, this chapter introduces stress and the issues relating to it. The reason why it is important to mention it sooner rather than later is because a lot of people suffer from stress. It may not affect you, but it's quite likely that at some point (if not already) you will work alongside, or get to know someone, who does. Stress is something that can happen to people who don't manage their time very well. It is also a direct consequence of the failure to adapt to change.

CHAPTER 2

Stress management: how it fits in

There isn't a definitive description of stress, because what one person finds stressful another might find acceptable or even pleasurable. If you asked ten people to define it, you would probably get ten different answers. But there are many ways of identifying stress.

This chapter identifies some common signs and symptoms of stress. It also describes situations where stress is likely to occur. It outlines some of the reasons why people suffer from stress or overwork, or feel overwhelmed. By becoming familiar with these, you will be able to add to what you have already learned about managing your time. Some suggested methods of dealing with stress will also be mentioned, but featured in detail later in the book.

Identifying stress

The word stress has been around for centuries, but not in the context in which it is used today. One of its original exponents was a seventeenth century inventor, an Englishman named Robert Hooke. He recorded the concept in his experiments to test the tolerance of load-bearing materials.

Today it is usually applied to humans who are certainly load-bearing entities. You can measure physiologically, as well as psychologically, the effects of applying too much stress. When most people talk about stress in individuals, the implication is a negative one. You hear people describing the effect of being "stressed out". But stress in certain circumstances may be seen as a positive phenomenon: the ability to harness internal resources to meet challenges and achieve realistic goals. (Note here that the emphasis is on the word "realistic".) If you are a fairly laid-back type, perhaps you do not carry enough stress.

> **Rookie Buster**
>
> When most people talk about stress in individuals, the implication is a negative one. You hear people describing the effect of being "stressed out".

It's quite usual to feel overwhelmed and unable to cope when there are just too many jobs needing to be done, and deadlines are looming. As stress begins to affect you, you feel suffocated and stifled. It's then that the balancing activities – socializing, hobbies, sports or simply "chilling out" – are needed more than ever. But so often when people are suffering from stress, they feel they must cut out such activities, for want of time. This is perfectly understandable, though extremely unwise. If you feel tired, drained and exhausted, you need to slow down or stop and look at what is causing you to feel stressed.

Positive vs. negative stress

But did you know that not all stress is bad? The opposite of "distress" is literally "eustress", from the Greek prefix "eu", meaning "well". The prefix "dis" or "dys" on the other hand carries a negative connotation. The words "dysfunctional" and "disapproval" are not likely to appear in a positive context. You are probably familiar with the word "euphoria" meaning a feeling of wellbeing. The antonym (word of opposite meaning) of that is "dysphoria", which is not so widely known.

The right amount of stress stimulates, whereas excessive stress destroys. Stress can therefore either be your friend or your enemy. Because stress can be a positive force, people sometimes forget that beyond a certain level it ceases to be healthy. Once you reach the point where it becomes negative, you must take some form of stress-busting action. At the correct level, stress releases hidden reserves of your creative energy. This allows you to operate at peak performance. You feel energized, motivated, confident, enthusiastic and in control.

> **Rookie Buster**
>
> Because stress can be a positive force, people sometimes forget that beyond a certain level it ceases to be healthy. Once you reach the point where it becomes negative, you must take some stress-busting action.

But perhaps you have experienced unacceptable levels of stress at some time or another? For short periods this is bearable. Should it become the norm, steps must be taken to deal with what can rapidly become burnout or "overwhelm". There could be a physical withdrawal from work or relationships because of excessive stress or dissatisfaction. It can quickly lead to exhaustion, irritability, depression and health problems.

Some people certainly are more prone to stress than others, but the statistics concerning stress as an illness are increasing. Insurance companies have (according to reports in the UK national press) seen a recent increase of 88 per cent in the number of claims made for loss of income owing to stress related issues. At the worst level, stress can actually kill you. But since you are reading this book, you need have no worries. Everything is under control (or it soon will be).

The message here is clear: positive stress is OK, while negative stress is not. To combat negative stress you must get a grip on your time management and develop a positive attitude. Once you stop yourself from being negative, it will prevent the stress increasing. Should you ever suffer from symptoms of stress, effective stress management is what's needed. This is an extension of time management. You must work out your own stress limits – keeping a diary will help.

> **Rookie Buster**
>
> Should you ever suffer from symptoms of stress, effective stress management is what's needed. This is an extension of time management. You must work out your own stress limits – keeping a diary will help.

A bit of self-analysis?

Here's a way of finding out how much stress you are carrying at the moment – answer Yes or No to the following questions. Where you've answered Yes, score the question with a figure between 0 and 10, depending on the stress rating you've given it.

1. Have you ever been landed with a huge piece of work, just a week before going on holiday? .... Yes/No
2. Is your company being forced to make redundancies? .... Yes/No
3. Do your colleagues behave unreasonably or unsympathetically? .... Yes/No
4. Is your boss refusing to support your bid for promotion? ... Yes/No
5. Do you regularly have to work evenings and weekends? ...... Yes/No
6. Are you made to feel awkward if you request time off? .... Yes/No
7. Have you had to miss out on a significant family event over the last 12 months due to work overload? .... Yes/No

8. In the last six months have you had to cancel a theatre visit/
concert/holiday/weekend away due to pressure of work? ....Yes/No
9. Do you regularly have sleepless nights because of work? .....Yes/No
10. Are you less decisive, is your memory unreliable,
do you lack concentration? .... Yes/No

If any of these issues relate to you, how many stress points do you score?

1) 0–40: You're OK.
2) 41–70: Be careful.
3) over 71: Watch out!

Depending on what your score is here, you will have to go back to planning and organization, just like with your time management. In your stress diary you should note how you feel on a daily basis so you can analyse the results. (Record whether you are happy/unhappy, unsettled, in control/out of control, anxious, frustrated, confident/nervous.) If you felt happy and on top of things, what were you doing when you felt like this? What factors influenced you? Had you been on your own or working alongside others?

Identifying the problem is vital. These clues will help you discover what makes you stressed. Also you may be able to see whether you are at risk of getting caught in an ever-decreasing spiral of working harder to attain success. This was mentioned in the previous chapter – false perceptions of good time management. Working harder, as discussed earlier, is simply not the issue. Spending longer and longer at work, your output actually decreases and you achieve less. Your sense of frustration increases along with your stress level. If one of the situations mentioned above is a common occurrence for you, you must try to change the way you work in order to avoid it happening too often.

What stress does

> **Rookie Buster**
>
> Stress is a state of feeling you are not in control. It carries with it an overwhelming belief that whatever you do, nothing will help.

Stress is used by the brain to deal with emergencies. In moments of crisis, people experience an adrenalin rush which prepares them for "fight" or "flight" mode. This is the great surge of energy which nature intended humans to use for self-preservation.

Today, the demand for increased productivity at work and the provision of more and more technology to "make it happen faster" is leading to "digital depression". Increasing numbers of employees are finding themselves on-call with the expectation that every phone call, text message or email warrants an immediate response. Stress is a state of feeling you are not in control. It carries with it an overwhelming belief that whatever you do, nothing will help.

In a recent survey conducted amongst employees, one in three attributed increased stress to technology. This condition has been diagnosed as "digital Darwinism" – an anxiety caused by the belief that an evolutionary process is taking place where only the most technologically up-to-date of humans will gain social and career success.

Some common sources of stress

Both negative and positive stressors can lead to stress. Some common categories and examples of stressors include:
- Sensory: pain, bright light.
- Life events: birth, death, marriage and divorce.
- Responsibilities: lack of money, unemployment.
- Illness: depression, obsessive compulsive disorder.

- Work/study: exams, project deadlines, group projects.

But why is it so important to be able to identify stress at work? Quite simply, because more staff absences are caused by stress than by the common cold. Stress begins as a buzz that keeps you on the go, operating effectively. It is that boost of nervous energy that gives you the ability to perform well. At its best, stress is pressure. At its worst, it is overload or burnout.

> **Rookie Buster**
>
> Adapting to stress is vital if you are going to overcome it. If you cannot manage your stress, it will overwhelm you and lead to anxiety and depression. Over a longer period of time, distress can lead to ill health.

The UK Health and Safety Executive (HSE) defines stress like this: "Stress is the reaction people have to excessive pressures or other types of demand placed upon them." Stress results when demands are too great or expectations are not met. The warning for business from the HSE is that stress is now the second biggest cause of work-related illness in the UK and therefore this issue needs to be urgently addressed. According to the HSE 150,000 workers have taken at least a month off work because of stress related illness.

Adapting to stress is vital if you are going to overcome it. If you cannot manage your stress, it will overwhelm you and lead to anxiety and depression. Over a longer period of time, distress can lead to ill health. In order that you don't become part of another statistic you are doing just the right thing – reading this book. But apart from that, if you are learning to manage your time, you must also effectively manage work-related stress.

When stress levels tip from positive to negative, people experience some of the following symptoms:

- Headache, indigestion, aching muscles.
- Disturbed sleep and fatigue.
- Change in appetite, increase in alcohol consumption or smoking.
- Loss of concentration, shortened temper, loss of self-esteem.

According to the *British Medical Journal*, chronic stress increases the risk of heart disease and depression. Stress can also weaken the immune system and make you less resistant to illness. Stress happens to individuals when too heavy demands are put on them or when expectations are not met. Most symptoms of individual and organizational stress are hidden below the surface (often referred to as the "iceberg syndrome"). It is only when signs such as irritability or headaches manifest themselves outwardly that other people become aware of these symptoms of stress.

If you can reduce the amount of stress you carry at work, it will result in:
- Reducing the likelihood of sickness and absence from work.
- Improving your performance.
- Enjoying better relationships with colleagues and customers.

Stress in the workplace

When related to an organization, stress shows itself by:
- Increased sickness absence.
- Significantly high staff turnover.

- Poor team and group working (e.g. role conflicts, interpersonal issues).
- Poor relationships with colleagues and clients.
- Back pain, RSI/upper limb disorders, bullying, harassment, poor performance.

Workplace stress rarely comes down to only one issue. It is a complex subject (like time management) comprising many strands. Going back to the iceberg analogy, most of an iceberg is hidden below the surface. It is just the same with work-related stress.

> **Rookie Buster**
> Workplace stress rarely comes down to only one issue. It is a complex subject (like time management) comprising many strands.

The best way of tackling the risk to employee health and organizational healthiness is to find the underlying issues below the surface. These develop in different ways and at different speeds and affect each individual with one or more symptoms.

While the elimination of stress from an entire organization is not always possible, it is possible to reduce drastically (and sometimes remove) stress from an individual. If you know what you are looking for, and have good strategies to put in place, you can reduce the risks of distress dramatically. Usually a combination of efforts in a number of different ways will be the most effective solution.

Individual stress vs. organizational stress

Work related stress is a health and safety issue of importance to everyone at work. If you are able to tackle the situations that produce the stress factors, it will have positive benefits for the company and all employees. You could be looking at stress which is endemic within the organization, or you could be feeling stress as an individual. Both are serious, but they need handling in different ways. For the purposes of this book, the focus is on the individual, not the organization.

Should you feel you are suffering from work-related stress, one of the most important things to do is to raise awareness of the issue by one or all of the following means:

- Start a dialogue, making others aware of the risks.
- Make positive suggestions.
- Identify any department which may have particular problems (this could include customer services, for example, if they are dealing with difficult clients).
- Encourage the company to carry out its own "workplace stress MOT".
- Explain the benefits, and the corporate responsibility for health and safety.

When considering stress and the individual, identifying the problem is essential. Sometimes however, people are not keen to admit that they are under pressure. They are worried that they will be judged harshly and looked upon as weak for not being able to cope. If you are stressed, you could be on the way to losing your perspective and your ability to focus. You also run the risk of incurring health problems. You must take action immediately. Otherwise you will get caught in the ever-decreasing circle of working harder to achieve success.

Some people don't know what to do, so they do nothing. They put up with an unsatisfactory situation, hoping that it will go away. But stress symptoms will not get better on their own.

Working harder (as explained earlier in the context of time management) is not the solution. It just won't help. Everything will take longer, and you'll achieve less. Alongside this your sense of stress and frustration levels will increase dramatically. If anyone where you work is showing any of the following signs, encourage them to seek help.

> **Rookie Buster**
>
> If you are stressed, you could be on the way to losing your perspective and your ability to focus. You also run the risk of incurring health problems. You must take action immediately. Otherwise you will get caught in the ever decreasing circle of working harder to achieve success.

Stress symptoms that should not be ignored

- Recurring headaches.
- Ringing in the ears or frequent noises in the head.
- Regular use of self-prescribed drugs.
- Palpitations and chest pains.
- Attacks of heartburn, stomach cramps, diarrhoea.
- Feeling that you may pass out.
- Getting any illness that is around.
- Loss of former concentration.
- Loss of former reliable memory.
- Difficulty in thinking around problems.
- Inability to reach satisfactory decisions.
- A feeling of being very low or dulled.
- A shut-down of all emotions except anger and irritation.
- Loss of sense of humour.
- Active love and caring have lessened.
- Tears or rage appear frequently for little reason.

Coping with stress

For decades, backache used to be the cause of most absenteeism from work. In the UK, stress now keeps up to a million people at home on an average day. Sickness absence – both long and short term – can mask other concerns besides stress, such as a poor work environment, bullying and other health issues. If you are concerned about a colleague who is suffering from stress, it is essential to find out what the underlying causes are. It could be much more than weak time management.

If you think that you have a problem, this is the first step towards dealing with it. Identify your symptoms and make an action plan. There are a number of ways you can set about reducing your stress levels. The most important is by learning to control your time – of course.

Rookie Buster

When learning how to deal with stress, one of the simplest strategies is to take control of what you can and ignore what you can't.

If you're overworked, sit down for a few moments and ask yourself what are the two most important things to be done today. What if nothing was done at all? What would the consequences be? Would it matter? Would it get done by someone else?

When learning how to deal with stress, one of the simplest strategies is to take control of what you can and ignore what you can't. Remember the phrase "Do your best and leave the rest." No one expects people to be perfect. When mistakes do occur, use them as opportunities to learn.

Coach's notes

This chapter explained how stress affects people, and how it impacts on your time management. If you are watching out for symptoms of stress, take steps to manage it if you think you already suffer from overwork. Here are ten tips for you:
- Pay attention to health related issues/stress symptoms.
- Define positive and negative stress situations that have affected you.
- Check your stress level as an individual – develop coping mechanisms.
- Use common sense.
- Look after your body.
- Control your mind.
- Keep an eye on your work/life balance.
- Be assertive where appropriate and take control.
- Take a break – even if it's only a few minutes away from your desk.
- Create your own personal reserve.

Now that you know a bit about the theory of time management and how to recognize stress, you are ready to move on to more practical aspects of dealing with both issues.

Go for it! Recognize that stress is positive up to a certain point. Beyond that, it can cause a reduction in output, depression, illness and absenteeism. If you are going to control or reduce stress, you must learn to manage it yourself. Fortunately it is not as hard as you might think. Effective stress management comes down to this: change the things that you can change, and don't worry about the things you can't change. As you become more able to manage your time effectively, you will find that you are less liable to suffer from stress.

Stress can be controlled by applying common sense – or the Pareto Principle (the 80/20 Rule). You can combat stress by looking after yourself – eating and sleeping sufficiently, taking regular exercise. You can also reduce your stress by taking steps to relax. In the meantime, don't worry – think about something calm and pleasant. Now, are you feeling a little better?

Notes

Before you can tackle time or stress management you will find it helpful to know what type of person you are. Work out what you do when you're at work and how you spend your time while you're there. Once you've done that, you will have a clearer idea of what's ahead of you in terms of getting to grips with your own time management. This chapter will help you identify the issues of overwhelm and disorganization which can hamper your effectiveness and productivity. It will also give you some exercises in self-awareness so that you will know how to access your personal strengths. This leads on to the sort of action plans which you can implement right away to start improving your time and stress management.

CHAPTER 3
Identifying your personal style

Overwhelmed and disorganized?

If you are keen to get to grips with your time management and control your stress levels, it is important that you know who you are, how you work, what comes easily to you and what seem to be uphill tasks. Do you, for example, when planning your day (you do plan your day, don't you?) choose routine tasks first? Or do you prefer to tackle difficult or unpleasant jobs right at the start, to get them out of the way? Perhaps you are creative and like to use your imagination in what you do. Or are you a "go with the flow" type of person, who matches performance to what is happening around you – you're calm if the workplace is calm, you get energized if everyone else is working at full speed?

Rookie Buster

If you are keen to get to grips with your time management and control your stress levels, it is important that you know who you are, how you work, what comes easily to you and what seem to be uphill tasks.

There are lots of other questions you should consider: do you find it difficult to focus on what you're doing? How easily distracted are you? Do you get carried away by something and realize it's long past your lunch break and you never even noticed? Are you a list-freak? Or do you hate putting things down on paper to remind you what should be done next? Do you know at what time of day you are likely to produce your best work? And do you use that time to carry out your most exacting tasks?

Learning to manage your time and stress better is fine, but it is a lot easier if you document how you spend your time and what makes you feel stressed. Surprisingly, most people don't have an accurate picture of how they spend their time. You may think you know how long you spend on each task, but if you wrote it down you would find your impressions would probably be inaccurate compared to the detailed time log. But first, let's spend a bit of time assessing you.

A bit of self-assessment

In order to improve something, you need to identify how it is now. This gives you an accurate starting point from which you can measure progress. It's also a way of finding out what needs changing or adapting. So let's begin by answering these questions.

1. I begin each day by making a daily task list............................Yes/No
2. I block out a chunk of time each day for each specific task (answering emails/backing up computer).....................Yes/No
3. Every three months I review my goals/objectives.................Yes/No
4. I rarely work late or at weekends..Yes/No
5. I delegate wherever possible...Yes/No
6. My telephone habits are good (audible/concise/prompt)...Yes/No
7. I have no difficulty preventing interruptions.......................Yes/No
8. I have learned how to say No...Yes/No
9. I usually finish all the tasks on my To Do list........................Yes/No
10. When dealing with people I usually get the result I want..Yes/No

If you've answered "Yes" to most of these questions, then you are well aware of time management habits and skills. If you have scored quite a few "No"s – carry on reading.

The reason you need to work out your personal strengths and weaknesses is so that you can use the best strategies to help you overcome your weak areas and start getting things done. If you use your natural energy you will achieve things faster. You should always reserve your high-performance hours for your most difficult task.

Rookie Buster

You should always reserve your high-performance hours for your most difficult task.

Everyone is different, but there are certain character types which give a clue as to how you might tackle your time management. Some people function well into the evening, yet have difficulty in making an early start. Others have no problem getting to their desk and firing up their computer at 6am because they are awake quite naturally and full of energy.

Do you have similarities with another type of person, often referred to as a "late tasker"? If you do, you'll find you produce your best work when there is a deadline looming. You work to optimum capacity when under pressure. If you've only got a couple of hours in which to do something, somehow your brain works brilliantly under these conditions. If you're driven to complete a task only when you have a time limit, you will have to impose your own deadlines, otherwise you may never get anything done.

Who do you think you are?

Here's another Q&A exercise – based loosely on the Belbin team roles which were the work of Meredith Belbin and researchers at Henley Management College near London, UK, quite a few years ago. Belbin and his colleagues found that after psychometric testing, different types of behaviour patterns emerged.

Tick the answer that best describes your response or behaviour:

1. I like to
   - [ ] work however late to finish a job
   - [ ] not worry about deadlines
   - [ ] work with someone/get help to finish
   - [ ] do what I want, but get the job done
2. I sometimes get upset when other people work more slowly than I do
   - [ ] Yes
   - [ ] No
3. I do my best work as part of a team/working with others by
   - [ ] showing great patience
   - [ ] pushing others to their limit
   - [ ] letting others set the priorities
   - [ ] setting work goals together
4. I like to help others with their work
   - [ ] Yes
   - [ ] No
5. When people come to see me at work
   - [ ] I like to chat with them
   - [ ] I let them sort out their own problems
   - [ ] I spend a lot of time listening to them
   - [ ] I become impatient
6. I constantly check to see how others are getting on with their work
   - [ ] Yes
   - [ ] No

7. When someone delegates a task to me, I prefer to
   - ☐ be given total responsibility
   - ☐ set early deadlines
   - ☐ plan to do the work with others
   - ☐ be patient
8. I prefer others to be in charge
   - ☐ Yes
   - ☐ No
9. I avoid wasting time by
   - ☐ getting through things quickly
   - ☐ showing concern for others
   - ☐ leaving others alone
   - ☐ rewarding others for their help/teamwork
10. I am always early for meetings
    - ☐ Yes
    - ☐ No
11. I encourage my friends/co-workers by
    - ☐ being friendly towards them
    - ☐ setting hard-and-fast deadlines
    - ☐ working as a team
    - ☐ avoiding conflict
12. Friendship is more important than deadlines
    - ☐ Yes
    - ☐ No
13. When my work schedule gets behind due to others, I feel
    - ☐ very stressed
    - ☐ concern for others
    - ☐ that it is someone else's fault
    - ☐ that the problem needs solving together
14. I plan my tasks way ahead of the deadline
    - ☐ Yes
    - ☐ No
15. I get added value in my work by
    - ☐ developing a network with other people
    - ☐ encouraging a relaxed atmosphere
    - ☐ using a team approach
    - ☐ stretching my team/co-workers
16. I always say thank you if someone has helped me
    - ☐ Yes
    - ☐ No

The score here isn't important. You need to find out whether you interact well with people or if you are more task-oriented, because that will have a bearing on how you manage your time. So, do you prefer getting on with the job or chatting with colleagues?

> **Rookie Buster**
>
> You need to find out whether you interact well with people or if you are more task-oriented, because that will have a bearing on how you manage your time.

Belbin defined three *action-oriented* roles: the Shaper, the Implementer and the Completer-Finisher.
1. The *Shaper* is dynamic and thrives on challenges and pressure.
2. The *Implementer* is disciplined and reliable, capable of turning ideas into practice.
3. The *Completer-Finisher* is painstaking and conscientious, inclined to worry. He finds delegating difficult, but always delivers on time.

Then there are the *people-oriented* roles: Co-ordinator, Team Worker and Resource Investigator.
1. The *Co-ordinator* is confident and authoritative, clarifies goals and takes decisions.
2. The *Team Worker* is co-operative, diplomatic and avoids confrontation.
3. The *Resource Investigator* is extrovert, communicates well and searches for opportunities and contacts.

Finally there are the *cerebral* roles: Plant, Monitor-Evaluator and Specialist.
1. The *Plant* is creative and imaginative and solves difficult problems but ignores incidentals and is poor at communicating.
2. The *Monitor-Evaluator* is strategic and discerning and sees all options but lacks the drive and ability to inspire others.
3. The *Specialist* is single-minded and dedicated, providing rare skills, but can only contribute on a narrow front.

Do you already have an idea which type best describes the way you work? Do you recognize any of your friends or colleagues from amongst this group? Have you got any idea which personality types from the three groups would be good at time management and who wouldn't? Perhaps some of these people would be more likely to suffer stress than others, too.

Have you noticed the shining example here out of all the personalities who is the perfect time manager? Of course, it's the Completer-Finisher. But he wouldn't be very good at keeping his stress levels under control. Does that mean you can't be good at both? This is something you will find out later.

Keeping a record

If you are ready to carry out a review of how you currently spend your time, the best and most accurate way to do it is to compile a time log. It shouldn't take more than 10 minutes a day to complete and you will probably need a further 20 minutes or so at the end of the week to analyse the results. Some professionals do this as a matter of course – lawyers, accountants, engineers, consultants – so that they can see at a glance on what projects or with which clients they have spent their time. The reason they use this method is for accounting purposes – imagine the headache involved when they need to apportion their time to see how much each client needs to be billed for their services. (If you can't see the point – pretend you have a charging rate of, say, $800 an hour. Under those circumstances wouldn't it be interesting to see how much you earned in a day?) One of the advantages of keeping a time log is that it will tell you, progressively, whether or not your time management action plan is working or not.

You need to divide your day into representative blocks of time – it could be 5-minute, 15-minute or half-hour intervals. However you record your time, remember to do it in real time. It is very difficult to be accurate if you are trying to remember what you did several hours earlier, particularly if you've had a busy day.

> **Rookie Buster**
>
> However you record your time, remember to do it in real time. It is very difficult to be accurate if you are trying to remember what you did several hours earlier, particularly if you've had a busy day.

At the end of the day you should conduct a simple analysis of the activities you've carried out. The four headings are: Priorities, Delegation, Time Wasters and Operations/Processes (this last heading can include managerial tasks as well if appropriate).

Priorities
These are the activities that represent genuine priorities for that working period. This should include only those tasks that make a significant contribution to what you are trying to achieve. Be firm in only identifying real priorities. These are by definition the few rather than the many tasks that you perform.

Delegation
This indicates those tasks that you could or should have given to someone else to complete. This also includes priority activities where appropriate. On consideration you may identify priority tasks that you could have delegated a significant part of, even if you needed to tackle another part of the work personally.

Time Wasters
Include here all the things that distracted you from your main objectives. These include interruptions, as well as those activities that (on reflection) you should have said no to. Time wasters are often insidious and yet when totalled up will often represent a significant part of the working day. Again, be disciplined when identifying time wasters. They are an essential component in gaining control over your working day.

Operations/Processes
This is by far the most difficult category to classify. Not everyone has a job that clearly includes such areas. But it is important for you to try to identify such tasks. Use an O for operational tasks and P for processes and systems. Operating refers to the technical or professional part of your job as well as the routine work, much of which could be delegated. Process tasks relate to work which is done through other people and includes such activities as planning, delegating work and reviewing results.

What's the score?

Analysing your time log will reveal a lot. It may show that there are some activities which you need to record in more detail. If, say, you identified that you spent a lot of your day sending emails, most of which was non-essential, you should break this down into more detail. How much was time-wasting and how much was applicable to the O/P category? Keep records of whether you were initiating the email or whether you were responding to incoming mail, who you were communicating with and how much of the time spent was actually productive.

Once you are happy with the classification of the day's activities, add up the number of time divisions you spent on each of the categories and factor it over the total divisions in the day. This calculation should provide you with two important pieces of information. First, are you investing enough of your time in areas that are essential to achieving your goals? Second, in which areas that are not essential to your goals are you spending too much time?

The result of keeping a log over a week is usually quite scary. You will probably find that you aren't spending much time on real priorities at all. It may also highlight how many of the activities that you are carrying out could be delegated to others. Don't be surprised if your time log reveals that a significant amount of your working day just disappears – used up by distractions and interruptions.

Rookie Buster

Don't be surprised if your time log reveals that a significant amount of your working day just disappears – used up by distractions and interruptions.

Now you've carried out this exercise, let's just recap. Further on you will find out the difference between an urgent and an important task (just like you learned the difference between being efficient and being effective). You will also discover how to use both the Pareto Principle and Parkinson's Law (which states that a task's perceived importance and complexity will grow in direct proportion to the time available for its completion) to your advantage, and the reason why time and stress management involve lots of words beginning with the letter D.

In summary

You've just spent some time working out what type of person you are and how you spend your day at the moment. Before moving on to practical applications for dealing with time and stress management, spend a few moments thinking about what you might like to change. It is often a good idea to start with the end in mind. What is it about having better time management and avoiding stress that would change your life forever?

Set yourself a challenge – work out exactly what your ideal day at work would be like. How much time are you going to devote to which task? You can multiply this for a week or a month, whatever is appropriate. Add to your list what events and/or people you are going to make sure no longer have the ability to raise your stress levels. Block out the anticipated amount of time you will spend on certain tasks, and work out how you can change your behaviour so that it eliminates stress or manages time better. It could be the way you behave with someone so that they cannot upset you so much. Maybe your boss always makes a point of giving you an urgent piece of work at 5pm on a Friday evening: go to see him earlier in the day and ask him if there's anything he needs you to do before the end of the day, as you have another urgent piece of work to finish and don't want to disappoint him. A change of tack may be all that is needed to bring about an improvement in his behaviour and in your stress level.

Rookie Buster

In terms of what you want to achieve, be realistic – you won't ever be perfect, but you will do better and have more control over your time and stress levels than you have at the moment.

In terms of what you want to achieve, be realistic – you won't ever be perfect, but you will do better and have more control over your time and stress levels than you have at the moment. If you know there's a big project looming and you're likely to put it off because you hate starting a complicated new piece of work, try a different approach. Perhaps this is where you suggest to your boss that you'd like to work on this from home. If he understands that your output may be greater in calm and uninterrupted surroundings, and his desire is to get the project under way as soon as possible under favourable conditions, he may well agree. It may take a bit of courage, but it's worth a try and if you don't ask, you'll never know.

> **Rookie Buster**
>
> Work with, not against, your personal strengths – if you ignore these you are wasting a valuable asset.

Coach's notes

Now you know a bit more about yourself and your style when it comes to work, you are ready to move on to the basic rules of time management. Some of the things covered in this chapter are essential when starting to take control of your time and monitoring your stress levels.

- Work out what sort of a person you are. How do you relate to people and tasks? Are you highly task aware, or are you more focused on people and relationships?
- When planning your day: do you choose the routine tasks first? Do you pick something you know you'll enjoy doing? Or do you try to get the difficult or unpleasant jobs out of the way early on?
- Do you know whether you are creative? Perhaps you prefer to "go with the flow"?
- Do you find it difficult to be focused on what is going on? Are you easily distracted by other people or events?
- Perhaps you are able to work late into the evening, when it is necessary to finish a task. Or do you wake up naturally early in the morning with an energy surge?
- With regard to lists, do you write a To Do list for each day? If so, what sort of jobs are left unfinished at the end of the day?
- Are you aware of your most productive hours of the day, when your mind works best? Do you try to get the most exacting jobs done during this time?

Go for it! Making time management work for you as an individual is important. At the very worst the alternative is to muddle on, feeling pressure and frustration, achieving the same amount (or less) than you actually wish to do. The purpose of going through the exercises in this chapter was to identify your personal strengths so that you could make use of them when dealing with time management and reducing stress. If you ignore what you can do naturally and easily, you are allowing circumstances (or other people) to control your life, and this often has an adverse effect.

Notes

This is where the work really begins. In this chapter you will learn the first steps towards developing your personal effectiveness strategy: managing your time and controlling your stress level. You will learn the essential things everyone should know about prioritizing and categorizing. You've learned about yourself, now you will spend time analysing the sort of work you do. Do you know how important each task is? Personal effectiveness encompasses both time management and controlling stress. It is possible to be a good time manager and not to suffer from stress, and the lesson starts now.

CHAPTER 4

Time and stress management: first steps

First things first

The golden rule when grappling with time management is having the ability to prioritize. If you can't prioritize, you can't manage your time or stress level. Why? Because you won't know when something is either urgent or important (or possibly both). If you don't know that, you won't know in which order to tackle jobs. So, let's begin with something you can put into practice straight away.

Are you familiar with the Urgency/Importance grid? This is essential knowledge if you want to classify the tasks you currently perform. It will help you get the best use of the time you spend on each type of work in the future.

A lot of people find they spend the greatest proportion of their time dealing with things that are urgent but not particularly important. One of the biggest pitfalls in time management is confusing urgency with importance when you are trying to prioritize. There are a number of factors that can change to make any one of your tasks more or less important, but time is not one of them. An unimportant job will remain an unimportant job – even if you've got an impossibly short deadline in which to deal with it.

Rookie Buster

One of the biggest pitfalls in time management is confusing urgency with importance when you are trying to prioritize.

You need to draw a grid like this:

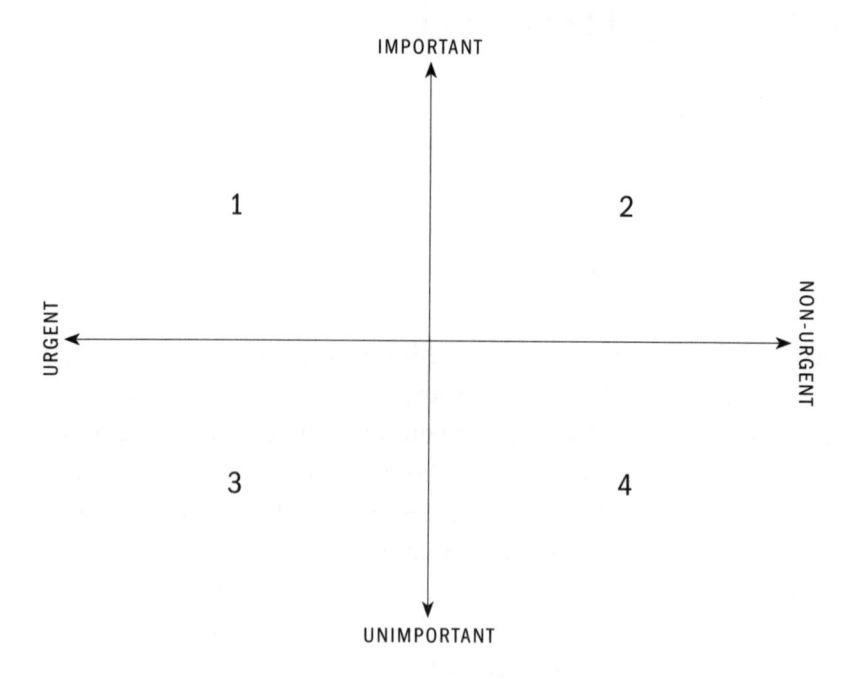

```
                    IMPORTANT
                        ▲
                        │
              1         │         2
                        │
    URGENT ◄────────────┼────────────► NON-URGENT
                        │
              3         │         4
                        │
                        ▼
                   UNIMPORTANT
```

and then work out which activities should be inserted where. These should be taken from your time log. Note the percentage of your time spent on each type of activity as well, if you want to be that specific.

Zone 1
These tasks are both important and urgent and are your No. 1 priorities. There is a risk that you will fail to plan these tasks properly because

of their urgency and then crisis manage them because of the stress you're suffering in order to complete them.

Any work that is both urgent and important requires immediate attention. You may have to clear your diary in order to meet a deadline and call in assistance from colleagues, giving all your attention to the aspects you have to control while delegating other parts to other staff. You need to make sure you are giving enough time to the job in view of its importance so that it can be done well.

Zone 2

Tasks that fall into this category are important but not urgent. This means there is probably no specific deadline, or it is still some way off. The danger here is if there is no deadline, you may never get around to doing them. You may on the other hand delay dealing with them until the deadline is looming and then crisis manage them to get them completed.

Jobs that are important but not urgent often fall off the chart. Some of the items are critical but because they have long deadlines – strategic planning, progress checking – and are complex ones, they are the most likely to be put on the back burner. In order to take control of these tasks, you may have to set aside specific times in which to deal with them – doing a bit at a time.

Zone 3

You should put tasks here that are fairly urgent but relatively low in importance. It is so easy to use up valuable time on these tasks because of their urgency. Ideally they should be completed adequately, but in a short time. You must remind yourself not to spend too much time on these jobs.

Zone 4

The jobs that fit here are neither important nor urgent. This makes them rather dangerous. But if you reduce the time you spend doing them you may find your working day less enjoyable. These things involve talking to people, doing pleasant but not very valuable stuff. If you cut them out altogether you could be distancing yourself from some of the softer aspects of the work environment and your colleagues could put pressure on you to break your resolve. You will have to be strict with yourself to avoid being tempted.

Learning your A, B, C

The next step is to categorize the tasks you have identified in your time log and from the grid. You must decide whether they are category A, B or C:

- Type A tasks are those which are important and urgent (zone 1 on the grid) – high stress.
- Type B tasks are either important or urgent, but not both (zones 2 and 3 on the grid) – medium stress.
- Type C tasks are those that are neither important nor urgent (zone 4 on the grid). They are routine – low stress.

A tasks
Try to complete a few of these urgent and important tasks each day. Mark them clearly as "A" tasks and if you aren't tackling them, work out why. If you don't tackle them, your stress level will go up.

B tasks
These are likely to take up the majority of your working day and there are usually lots of "B" tasks.

C tasks
These low-priority tasks should be fitted in to your time management plan as and when your schedule allows.

When it comes to scheduling tasks into the working day, we should follow these guidelines:

A typical working day will include a mixture of A, B, and C tasks. Don't expect to work through all the A tasks, followed by the B tasks and so on. It is better if you have periods of great concentration, followed by periods where less demanding tasks are dealt with.

Rookie Buster

A typical working day will include a mixture of A, B, and C tasks. Don't expect to work through all the A tasks, followed by the B tasks and so on. It is better if you have periods of great concentration, followed by periods where less demanding tasks are dealt with.

Everyone has performance fluctuations during the working day. At certain times you are likely to be more effective and energetic than others. (This was something you looked at in the previous chapter.) Provided you are aware of your own style and cycle you can implement the most intensive tasks at the optimum times of your alertness. This is a great asset towards personal effectiveness and controlling stress levels.

Don't forget – it's very easy to confuse urgency with importance when you are trying to identify your priorities. An unimportant job will remain unimportant even if the deadline is impossibly short. It's best to get these jobs out of the way as soon as you can. The Urgency/Importance grid is a great way to kick-start your time and stress management because it helps you *classify* tasks so you can *clarify* your priorities.

Rookie Buster

The Urgency/Importance grid is a great way to kick-start your time and stress management because it helps you classify tasks so you can clarify your priorities.

The 4 D Approach

There is another effective method for tackling procrastination. This is known as the 4 D Approach. In order to avoid putting things off, you make a rule to deal with things using one of the four "D" words.

1. Delay reaction (not the task)
Stop and think for a few moments if you are being asked to take on a job that (a) you really shouldn't be doing, (b) you don't really know how to do, or (c) you don't have time for and are therefore likely to put off doing it. Is the task you are about to commit to something you know enough about? Have you been briefed (at all)? Were you asked to do the job by someone else who didn't understand it? Problems often occur at the briefing stage. If in doubt, delay reaction. Say that you cannot make an informed judgement in a rush. Hasty decisions are often regretted and you are more likely to procrastinate about tackling it if you're in any doubt. You should not agree to take something on for inadequate or the wrong reasons. This is one of the quickest ways of getting stressed.

2. Diary decision
Block out space in your diary, or daily planner, so that you can see there is space for a job to be done. If you want to avoid delay, this is one way of removing the "I haven't got time" excuse. It reinforces the importance of tackling the job. If you keep being reminded every time you look in your diary or planner that on Friday morning you're going to start this work, you are much more likely to stick to it. The event is being reinforced in your subconscious and the seeds of a "just do it" habit are being formed.

Equally, if there is a big job that needs to be started, you should plan to spend an hour a day dealing with it. Rather than having to write a huge report all in one go, why not spend a little time each day for two weeks pulling it together? This is a far less painful way of getting it done. It is the same as "chunking". A task that is daunting by virtue of its size can best be dealt with in small sections. The answer to the question "What is the best way to eat an elephant?" is "Cut it into bite sized chunks."

3. Delegate

Maybe one of the reasons you aren't able to tackle a job you've put off for ages is that it really isn't one that you should be dealing with anyway. Perhaps you agreed to do it to try to be helpful. But stop for a moment and think it through. Enlist the help of others to take over aspects of the task if that is possible. A problem shared is sometimes halved and two brains may be better than one.

If the job is something that could be done better by someone else entirely, then delegate it completely to the best skilled person. If outsourcing is a suitable solution, then consider taking that step.

4. Deadline

This is the final suggestion, if you've tried all the other steps. You know what you're taking on, because you found out all about it before you said "yes". Now you must mark out the time to deal with it and "just do it". The best sort of deadline is one that is realistic. If you set a ridiculously short deadline, you will more than likely fail to achieve it. Find out the real deadline and plan your work accordingly. You won't enjoy it or do it well if the deadline is impossible.

One way to make yourself feel good and to avoid getting stressed is to try to finish the task a little ahead of schedule. This will allow you a bit of time to go over the work and check it.

These suggestions are just a start, and there is more advice to come. Don't forget, one of the biggest hurdles to personal effectiveness, time management and controlling stress is the desire to put something off if you're not all that keen to do it. Dealing with priorities is a very important first step. If you can try to practise this each day, however much of an effort it may be at first, it will become progressively easier.

Rookie Buster

Dealing with priorities is a very important first step. If you can try to practise this each day, however much of an effort it may be at first, it will become progressively easier.

More suggestions on procrastination and how to overcome it

Putting off jobs you dislike doing is something everyone does. Unfortunately, most jobs that are put off don't go away. They remain, waiting to be done, and they tend to stay at the back of your mind (or the bottom of your To Do list). They can make you feel rather guilty when you remember them, but you still don't get on and tackle them.

If you become rather good at putting jobs off (because you think it's good time management) it can have a big disadvantage. It tends to lead to an ever-increasing number of jobs that remain outstanding. That list starts growing dramatically and then as the list gets longer it becomes even more difficult to make a start on any of them.

It is unlikely that you will ever get around to dealing with these things if you bunch them all together and keep thinking you'll deal with them when you have a "spare moment". Bundling, bunching, batching tasks – whatever you want to call it – can be an effective form of time management, but not in this case. If you've got loads of unpleasant tasks piling up, there is only one way to deal with them and that is – the sooner the better. Zap them – and you will find you feel much better and less stressed, if you can see the list growing shorter each day.

There's such a lot to be said about procrastination it could take up a huge chunk of this book. If you have a problem starting certain jobs or you put them off over and over again, you may have to change the way you feel about certain tasks to enable you to deal with them.

Rookie Buster

If you have a problem starting certain jobs or you put them off over and over again, you may have to change the way you feel about certain tasks to enable you to deal with them.

Do the worst job first

Doing the worst job first involves making a real effort to get the worst task out of the way as soon as possible. Don't allow anything to deflect you from your intention. A task you don't want to do can become an ongoing source of stress and anxiety. This in turn leads to a loss of effectiveness, which will continue until the job is tackled.

Big jobs can best be done bit by bit

This may be the only way to get on with long-term tasks when you can't see past them because they are so enormous. Breaking a big job into bits will allow you to get some of it out of the way. This small amount of success will improve the way you feel about it, and this should improve your motivation. Continue, and you will get through to the end. Making a series of smaller commitments is much easier than making a single large one. If you can assign a deadline to each "bit" you will find that short-term targets are easier to keep. ("I'll get this chapter finished by the end of the week" is more achievable than saying "I'll complete the book by the end of September.") It also gives you the chance to correct things if there is any slippage, or changes that need to be made as you go along.

Going public

Making a public commitment is one way of making sure you deal with a job you're reluctant to start. You could go into print and circulate a note to colleagues saying what you are proposing. Alternatively you could mention it at a meeting where other colleagues are present so that you know you have witnesses to the statement, always assuming you would be embarrassed if you failed to complete the task by the deadline.

Doing your homework

Perhaps you plan your work activities the night before, either the last thing before you leave work, or during the evening. Planning tomorrow's jobs the night before is effective because it avoids you getting distracted when you arrive at work. If you identify a task you want to get on with first thing in the morning, you will make a commitment to achieve something positive at the start of the day. That motivates you to continue to work effectively and you may achieve more than you'd anticipated.

Coach's notes

The most important rules in time management relate to procrastination and prioritizing. If you learn how to avoid putting things off and work out what jobs should be done first, everything else should fall into place. If you are prone to procrastination and aren't sure how to prioritize, this chapter should help you overcome it.

- It is a mistake to think that a job gets easier if you leave it. Actually the reverse is true.
- Make sure you incorporate your A, B and C tasks into your To Do List. "A" tasks are the absolute musts; "B" tasks are less urgent, but still important; "C" tasks are nice when you can get around to them.
- If you're struggling to cope. try bundling tasks together. You can earmark an hour in the day for making phone calls, or emailing. This gets things done in chunks.
- Reward yourself. Enjoy the sense of achievement as you get to grips with your time management.

Go for it! Have you got a handle now on how to prioritize? One quick tip: if you were leaving the country for an indefinite period and had time to do only five things – what would they be? Have you learned the difference between an urgent and an important task? Urgent tasks should be dealt with first and quickly. Important jobs are not always speedily resolved and can take longer. Do you know one of the main reasons for procrastination? Fear. Don't put off a task because it seems too big or too daunting. Tackle it anyway – a bit at a time.

Notes

Chapter 4 set out the first important steps towards gaining control of your time. These were: identifying what your priority tasks are, and tackling the tendency to procrastinate. Now you can begin to formulate an action plan which is tailored specifically to your goals. This is based on the key issues which, if not addressed, can waste time while raising stress levels. You will learn to evaluate how busy you are – think about *tasks* versus *time*. It is all too easy to measure activity when you should in fact be measuring the outcome. Good time management means working out what action produces the best result. Do not confuse "busyness" with "output".

CHAPTER 5

Formulating an action plan

Rolling out your action plan

One of the most important time management skills is the ability to identify and define your goals clearly. If you already have clear ambitions and aspirations, you may not find this difficult to do. But there are many people who fail to achieve what they wish because they are unable to set goals and monitor their achievements as they progress. One of the main barriers to turning ambitions into achievements is being "reactive" in day-to-day tasks. If you cannot be "proactive" in your approach to tasks, you are limited in your ability to make things happen.

Reactive vs. proactive

At work there is often a lot of organizational pressure to be responsive and short term in your thinking, with instant reaction and quick results. This quickly crushes any imaginative approach you may have, as it makes heavy demands on people. Reactive work is driven by events and other people. This alone can cause time management issues and raise stress levels to an unhealthy point. At work most people tend to do what they get rewarded for. In a climate where "instant gratification" is the required norm, there is rarely room for a "proactive" attitude.

If you can be proactive, it is possible to have far better time management than if you are reactive. There is in fact a huge difference. Anticipating events and being in a position to take appropriate action when the right moment arrives is manageable, but reacting to a crisis is stressful and fraught with difficulty because you are not in control of events. Proactive people look ahead and predict the likely outcome of events as they unfold.

In time and stress management terms, be proactive wherever possible, because by doing so you will achieve greater outcomes and keep stress levels to a minimum. Keep your eyes ahead of you or looking upwards, rather than downwards. The view is so much more interesting.

Rookie Buster

In time and stress management terms, be proactive wherever possible, because by doing so you will achieve greater outcomes and keep stress levels to a minimum.

Proactive techniques

1 Brainstorming

One of the most effective time management skills for identifying goals is to brainstorm. Blue-sky thinking is popular and can be done alone, or with colleagues, as part of a project team or department – whichever is appropriate to the task in hand. The aim might be to produce ways of speeding up a particular process, or identifying areas for business development when faced with a downturn in the economy. You can generate as many ideas as possible – they don't have to be researched, analysed or discussed at this stage.

This process might throw up such ideas as: improving customer loyalty; reducing costs of after sales service; introducing induction training for new staff; addressing issues of staff turnover; competitor analysis; maintaining a competitive edge; and new technology.

The ideas here could be developed by means of a SWOT analysis – comparing Strengths, Weaknesses, Opportunities and Threats.

2 Goal definition

To continue the proactive approach, select a couple of ideas that you feel able to take forward and turn them into reality by linking them to specific deadlines. A goal isn't really a goal if it doesn't have a deadline. (Do you remember those tasks which were important but, because they had no time limit on them, never got done?) Most people make New Year's Resolutions, but how many fall by the wayside because there is no realistic time limit? If you can incorporate the SMART principle here, you are far more likely to achieve your objective:

Specific
Measurable
Achievable
Realistic
Time related

Rookie Buster

A goal isn't really a goal if it doesn't have a deadline.

In time management terms, turning an aspiration into a goal is a process. Goals need specific targets, which dictate how you manage your day. Goals also help you achieve output. In order to achieve your goals (which lead you to attaining your aspirations) you may have to change the way you do things, and dump some old time-wasting habits.

Without a clear sense of direction (being proactive) you will drift into short-term (reactive) output – being efficient, but falling far short of your desired goal. This prevents long term effectiveness. One of the key things if you want to be a good time manager is recognizing the differences between being reactive and efficient (taking limiting actions), and behaving in a proactive and effective way (taking far-reaching actions). Be sure to make this important distinction, and take steps to do the latter, not the former.

3 Deciding your objectives

You may have set a clear goal as a result of your proactive approach to work, but you won't achieve it without clearly defined objectives. (Refer to the SMART criteria on the previous page – remember that goals have to be Achievable.) You have to be able to measure things accurately to work out (a) what needs to be done, (b) how you're going to do it, and (c) decide how it will work. For example, if you want to increase the number of customers you have in a particular market sector because economic factors indicate this is a growth area, you would need to:

- Set a time by which this percentage increase is to be achieved.
- Decide on the research and operational methods to achieve it (e.g. increased advertising in trade journals, taking a stand at an exhibition specifically related to that sector).

Once you've decided on a Specific objective and limited the amount of Time in which you have to achieve it, the methods you use to get there become Relevant and Measurable.

Formulating an action plan

> **Rookie Buster**
>
> Once you've decided on a Specific objective and limited the amount of Time in which you have to achieve it, the methods you use to get there become Relevant and Measurable.

4 Order of priority

Back to prioritizing again – it is one of the key time management skills. You've set the goals and decided on the objectives, but unless they are realistic, you won't achieve them. Objective grading is crucial to the outcome, so you need to select them in order of importance. Keep in mind practical issues – for example, are any of the objectives dependent on outside influences? These could be other people or seasonal constraints relating to certain products – you may have to wait before putting your ideas into practice in this case.

Once you are ready to go, it helps to keep yourself on track (in terms of time management) if you announce what you are doing and when you will have a result. If you make this sort of commitment it doubles the likelihood that you will achieve your goal. Things sometimes go wrong, despite careful planning, but under those circumstances you would be able to review the results (or lack of them) to find out quickly where things failed, or were unrealistic. Perhaps one of the outside influences, beyond your control, did not materialize.

5 Time specific

This is the final part of the SMART acronym. When being proactive, you still need to keep an eye on the main day-to-day tasks. If you spend all your time on your new schemes and fail to pay attention to the routine jobs, you could find yourself doing a spot of "crisis management" and having to react to a situation. So not only do you need to factor in your habitual tasks, but you must also be creative in planning time for your far-reaching objectives. Few people even take the time to plan each day what they want to achieve the next day. But don't limit it to a 24- or 48-hour period. If you are being proactive, you could work much further ahead. Create a monthly plan, a long term goal, or a vision for the future which could be years ahead. One of the important things to do to keep your proactive thinking on track and avoid reactive behaviour is to be able to ban interruptions. There is advice on how to acquire this skill in Chapter 6.

Become a planning expert

It is often said that the quickest way to do a lot of things is to do one thing at a time. This relates to planning, and if you don't plan, you are actually planning to fail. People who want good time management and low stress in their life know how to plan.

Just to recap: you've learned about proactive and reactive behaviour and the way they affect what you can achieve. It's also useful to be able to distinguish between "Progress Tasks" and "Maintenance Tasks". A *progress* task is one which you know will move you towards a position which is better than the one you are in now. A *maintenance* task is one which allows you only to get to a position which is equal to the one you were in before. There is nothing worse than running at full speed and staying in the same place.

Rookie Buster

A progress task is one which you know will move you towards a position which is better than the one you are in now. A maintenance task is one which allows you only to get to a position which is equal to the one you were in before.

In relation to planning objectives – how far should you go?

Some people like to have a *strategic* plan. This is one that encompasses long term company and organizational objectives. Obviously you would need to identify specific goals in order to make it achievable, and establish priorities including listing all the tasks involved. You would probably have to review it regularly, streamline it, implement it in stages, evaluate it and make it a continuous process. But this sort of planning is proactive behaviour at the highest level.

The next level of proactive thinking is to plan for the *medium term*. These objectives would not be quite so far reaching or aspirational. They would be goals that are important rather than urgent, but would need to be set to specific deadlines to be realistic.

The tasks involved could be broken down into segments – some of which could be delegated. If you are faced with a complex job, always try to cut it into more manageable sub-divisions. These medium term plans need to be reviewed against the strategic plan regularly, to see that they are complementary to it, not competing against it.

Is it possible to set *short term* goals which are proactive, not reactive? Of course. There is nothing wrong with a weekly plan. At the beginning of each week, allocate time to plan your weekly action list. This is a list of the top-ranking important tasks to be carried out during the next five days. As it is a fairly short time frame, make sure your allocation of hours required to carry out the tasks is accurate. If your anticipated timing is unrealistic, your planning, however well intentioned, will fail.

On a *daily* basis, your plan should be strict, particularly with regard to allocation of time spent. Always go back to basics where you can – defining the list of tasks in order of urgency and importance. Number and prioritize these things as accurately as you can. If possible, factor in a bit of slack – just in case things slip and you need longer to accomplish something. There is nothing worse than "over-scheduling" your time – finding that you have minus 10 minutes to get to a meeting at a venue halfway across town. Over-scheduling is depressing and self-defeating.

Another important thing to remember is that it is best to allow yourself to finish one task before starting the next one. Juggling work is sometimes unavoidable, but it denies you the satisfaction of crossing a job off the list when it is completed. If you are really pushed for time, you could always try rescheduling a task you're unlikely to complete to further ahead in the day or week. But if a task has to be shifted, make sure it becomes the next day's No. 1 priority task.

Rookie Buster

If you are really pushed for time, you could always try rescheduling a task you're unlikely to complete to further ahead in the day or week. But if a task has to be shifted, make sure it becomes the next day's No. 1 priority task.

The ratio of effort to time

Are you familiar with the effort to time ratio? This works on the basis that the more effort that you put into a complex task in its early stages, the greater the amount of time you will save at the end. Early preparation in any project leads to better organization (whether it is just you doing the job or a group of people involved). It also means that you are working proactively, and avoiding the likelihood of any reactive behaviour. Put in as much effort as is required to avoid blame, doubt, recrimination – and at worst (if things really go pear-shaped) litigation. It will keep everyone's stress levels within an acceptable range.

By working hard at the beginning of each new task or project, you will be far less stressed. The greatest input is always in the early stages, and as the project progresses, the amount of effort required to keep it going usually decreases. If this isn't the case, you may find that the required effort in the early stages wasn't forthcoming, which is why there is last minute "reactive" behaviour – otherwise known as crisis management.

Rookie Buster

By working hard at the beginning of each new task or project, you will be far less stressed. The greatest input is always in the early stages, and as the project progresses, the amount of effort required to keep it going usually decreases.

Coach's notes

If you are keen to work smarter rather than harder, which all good time managers should be, it is worth bearing the following points in mind. In order of importance they are:

- **Avoid procrastination – do it now**

  Don't put off doing something that must be done. If it really needs sorting it may be possible to do it quickly. (If your office building is on fire, you can ring the emergency services in a few seconds. It may take longer to put the fire out, but that is thankfully not your job.)

- **Learn to prioritize**

  Identify the three most important tasks and work at them until they are completed. Enjoy the sense of achievement in marking them "Done". If you can't decide – pretend you are going to the Moon and you only have time to do three things before you leave Earth.

- **Why be perfect?**

  You don't have to do everything. Leave things that will really look after themselves to do so – never micro manage. Remember the Pareto Principle (the 80/20 Rule) – sometimes almost perfect is good enough. Good time managers know this is true.

- **Be proactive rather than reactive**

  Actively manage the future before it happens. Decide what is important to you and what you want to achieve. Take a raincoat with you, and the sun will probably shine all day.

- **Do one thing at a time**

  And finish it before starting the next – don't get pushed into doing something unexpectedly. Delay saying "Yes" if you find it hard to say "No". Be vague, or let your voicemail take the strain.

- **Get organized**

  Clear any backlog and get rid of unwanted clutter, whether it's tasks that are never likely to get done or paperwork that you'll never need or read. Remember the "D" words: Deal with it, Delegate it, Deposit it or Discard it.

Go for it! These are useful rules when coping with managing your time and controlling your stress. The more familiar you become with how to plan your work and work your plan, the easier your time management will become. If you can remember the effort to time ratio, it will help you get through complicated work more easily. Don't forget the difference between being proactive and being reactive. Proactive behaviour is much more positive than reactive actions. Think about how you could change outcomes by working at staying in control. Always work smarter rather than harder – it makes sense.

Notes

Notes

This chapter looks at one of the most important skills for good time management. The ability to deal with interruptions effectively is essential. When you are concentrating on the main demands of a job, an interruption will stop you in your tracks. You then deal with the crisis or job that has arisen. This erodes time allotted for the job you are doing and interferes with your train of thought. The net result is further loss of time as you try to get back to the task in hand. If you've ever used the sheer volume of interruptions you've suffered as justification for your lack of achievement, pay careful attention to what comes next. Unfortunately people are the main cause of interruptions, so it involves handling colleagues appropriately.

CHAPTER 6

Dealing with interruptions

Saying "No" to interruptions

Did you know that on average someone is interrupted from their work every seven minutes? This could be because of the phone ringing, the email alert flashing on your computer screen, someone coming to speak to you, or many other causes. Do you find yourself working "in between disturbances"? Have you ever used the number of interruptions you've received as an excuse for not finishing a piece of work on time? Interruptions can account for about a quarter of your working day, which is fairly shocking. If you don't know how to handle such hindrances to your progress, you will find it difficult to get on with important work that requires your full concentration.

You've read in an earlier chapter how easy it is to confuse being busy with working effectively. If you're interrupted while doing some painstaking work, you are likely to abandon the task in hand, temporarily, to crisis manage the urgent issue. This has the effect of cutting your productivity. One suggestion that can help is to "bundle" or "batch" interruptions to a certain part of the day. If they *can* wait, then this is a good ruse. But if they cannot, you need to find ways of avoiding interruptions. One way of doing that is by saying "No". If you do what you've always done, you'll get what you've always got. So when it comes to working effectively, you should work harder at doing fewer things. Less can sometimes lead to so much more.

> **Rookie Buster**
> If you do what you've always done, you'll get what you've always got. So when it comes to working effectively you should work harder at doing fewer things. Less can sometimes lead to so much more.

When faced with numerous interruptions throughout the working day, it is vital to be able to spot what the interruption represents as a demand on your time. Does this sound like familiar territory? Remember the importance of distinguishing an urgent from a non-urgent task? You cannot avoid dealing with an urgent interruption, but if you are faced with a non-urgent one you must be able to defer it, in a polite but clear manner.

Interruptions during the working day not only take up time, but the secondary impact is the amount of time it takes to get back into what you were doing before the interference occurred. No one should ignore important or urgent interruptions, but neither should you feel guilty about avoiding unimportant demands on your time.

> **Rookie Buster**
> No one should ignore important or urgent interruptions, but neither should you feel guilty about avoiding unimportant demands on your time.

There are a number of strategies you can employ to reduce the time lost to interruptions. One example is to use a gatekeeper (a secretary, assistant or messaging service if you have one) to act as a screening system. You could, if you want to be helpful, tell people when you are available to speak to. This would mean setting aside a certain time of day or day of the week and sticking to it. Hopefully you won't find too long a queue of people waiting for you at that appointed hour.

It is not being suggested that you should ignore everything and everyone. You need to maintain good relationships with your boss, colleagues and staff, so accessibility is a requisite. It should not, however, be at the expense of *your* time and just when *they* feel like it. The process works best when it is two-way. If someone comes rushing up to you asking for some of your time, the best way to deal with it is to find out exactly why they need you, and whether or not what they want has to be sorted immediately. If not, then it can wait. But it is always polite to suggest another time when you will be able to help them and give the matter your undivided attention.

Unsolicited visits from colleagues at unscheduled times are most unhelpful when you are striving to manage your time effectively. You need to develop a clear but polite way of telling them when you are too busy to be interrupted.

Classifying interruptions

When you created your time log, you must have become aware of the common interruptions that erode your day and bring your work to an abrupt halt. Make sure you are aware of the type of interruptions you face on a regular basis, and of who and/or what causes them and how much time they take up. Once you've collected this information, have a look to see if any patterns are visible.

Rookie Buster

Make sure you are aware of the type of interruptions you face on a regular basis, and of who and/or what causes them and how much time they take up. Once you've collected this information, have a look to see if any patterns are visible.

Work out the following:
1. How much time did you spend on interruptions this week?
2. How many were important?
3. How many were unavoidable?
4. What were the main causes?
5. Were they mostly people-related rather than to do with things (e.g. equipment and technology)?
6. Is there any familiar pattern occurring?

Until you have a clear idea of what causes the interruptions, you cannot begin to develop skills to control them.

Here's a quick list for you to consider:
- If it's mainly the telephone, switch on your voicemail.
- If you spend too much time talking on the phone, limit yourself to five minutes per call (buy a timer, if you need to).
- If you're regularly confronted by colleagues coming up to you or walking past your workstation, develop some negative body language (avoiding eye contact, not turning to face people when they speak to you).

- If they aren't susceptible to hints, keep looking at your watch.
- Keep people standing, and you should stand up too.
- If all else fails, wear headphones and become selectively deaf.

This new time and stress management skill that you need to practise is: Elimination. Saying or conveying the message "No". You can probably recall a number of occasions when you tried to make contact with someone and they put you off (politely) by not engaging with you. This may not come easily to you, but, like most new habits, it will become less of an effort in time. Learning how to cope with interruptions requires tenacity. Do stick with it – you won't get anywhere if you find it hard to do and so abandon any attempt after a few days.

Rookie Buster

Learning how to cope with interruptions requires tenacity. Do stick with it – you won't get anywhere if you find it hard to do and so abandon any attempt after a few days.

Now here are nine important techniques for managing interruptions and keeping focused:

1. Try very hard – and this will be difficult at first – *not to do* three things each day; in other words, say "No" to three things. Don't react just because someone says you should (or you think you should fall in with their plans). How can you, if you're a junior member of staff for instance, actually say "No" to a superior asking you to do something? One way is by finding out straight away if it is an overriding and urgent matter that would require you to abandon whatever other task you are engaged in. Don't indicate that you are unwilling to accept their request, but, as you cannot complete both tasks, ask which one your boss feels should take precedence. (This is back to prioritizing – in the context of handling interruptions – coupled with a bit of assertive behaviour.)

2. Message taking: surely everyone can do this without any training? But you'd be surprised at how something which should be time saving often turns out to be the opposite. As with everything, there is a right and a wrong way to do it. If someone has offered to take messages for you to save your time, make sure they get the right information in a clear and concise way. A huge amount of time is wasted deciphering arcane notes or cryptic clues, whether you are the transmitter or the receiver. When taking a message, here is what needs to be done:
   - Write down the caller's name and telephone number and the time at which they called.
   - Repeat name and contact number back to check it is written it correctly.
   - Read back any message that has been left.
   - Ask if the matter is urgent.
   - Check what action is required (e.g. caller to be rung back/will call again).
   - Make a note of the caller's mood (e.g. angry, worried, upset).
   - Write legibly if not using email to forward information.
   - Pass on to person promptly.
   - If possible check that they received it.
3. If you're faced with a big job which needs to be completed in a fairly short space of time, there is another tactic you could try. You might negotiate with your employer that you complete the work at home. This is in effect creating an interruption-free zone. Explain that this would dramatically increase the amount of work you'd get done and have other knock-on advantages. You could tell him that you'd be able to complete the work in three days from home, whereas you're fairly certain that working at the office it might take five or more. There's no doubt that most people can achieve the amount they would normally manage at the office in, say, a quarter of the time when working in an uninterrupted way. Is this something you would be prepared to try? It can save hours of time if you can bargain for some flexible working.

> **Rookie Buster**
>
> Don't become a slave to email. It may be considered polite to respond to an email quickly, but replying immediately is usually not necessary.

4. When dealing with interruptions – are you allowing them to happen? This is one that you may be imposing on yourself directly. Don't become a slave to email. It may be considered polite to respond to an email quickly, but replying immediately is usually not necessary. You're not being efficient if you check your emails twenty times a day. In fact recent research has shown that people who respond instantly to email are either stressed or have low self-esteem. If you can manage your time well and don't allow your stress level to become raised, you are part of the relaxed majority who don't permit emails to exert any pressure on your time. You may feel "driven" to empty your email in-box on a regular basis, but when you allow messages to distract you from important work, take control and say "No, not now – later." You can also become an expert at un-subscribing to emails from non-essential senders. This helps to limit the amount of unwanted mail that arrives in your in-box on a regular basis. Make sure your spam filter is up to date and that other unwanted messages are blocked.
5. Exercise the closed door rule (only effective if you have a door – and there are a lot of open-plan offices these days). Apart from when you actually want to encourage people to come into your office or workspace, keep your door closed. A door wouldn't prove an effective barrier to someone who has an important reason to see you. But then, you should always make time for someone who really needs you. A door does, however, act as a good deterrent to those who are just passing by and may have a trivial request to make.
6. Sociable colleagues who prefer talking to working are great to have around – except when you are really busy. Most organizations have

some of these people and they are almost the biggest time wasters of all. If you are faced with the problem of trying to cut down the chatter so you can step up your work, suggest a time for a chat which suits you. It might be in your lunch or coffee break, or after work. Alternatively you could arrange to see them in their workspace rather than them coming to see you. The advantage here is that if you go to them, it's a lot easier to leave them than trying to get them to leave you.

> **Rookie Buster**
> Sociable colleagues who prefer talking to working are great to have around – except when you are really busy.

7. Keep control of meetings. Meetings are an excellent way to waste valuable time, unless you are smart and organized. Although they are sometimes unavoidable, it is essential to make them as short as possible. If you need an agenda, work it out beforehand and stick to it. Be assertive and ask "How long is this likely to take?" If you have allowed an hour to see someone, make sure you turn up at the pre-arranged time and place, adhere to your time limit and don't allow others, or yourself, to over-run. Once you've developed this habit, you'll be surprised how other busy people will respect you for your self-discipline. Being known for your effectiveness at handling meetings will enhance your reputation.

8. Deal with unsolicited requests and invitations. If people ask you to do things or attend meetings or conferences and so on, there is a way to combat these unsolicited demands on your time. You need to be ruthless and decide what you need to do, rather than what you would like to do (if time permits). You must be firm and ask yourself: could someone else attend on your behalf and get the same result? Would there be any direct benefit to you (or your organization) if you attended personally? Networking is an important and

valuable skill, and if opportunities arise they should not always be passed over. However if there is no discernible advantage in attending a function, other than out of politeness or a sense of duty, decline. If you don't do this you will have blown a hole in your interruption avoidance strategy. Note that when saying "No" it is important to reject the request, not the requestor.

> **Rookie Buster**
>
> When saying "No" it is important to reject the request, not the requestor.

9. Creating a buffer zone is another simple and effective way of dealing with interruptions. If you find it difficult, make an appointment (with yourself) to have a bit of thinking time. Blocking out part of your day for thinking is positive and helpful. During that time, make sure you ignore emails, telephone calls and personal visits from colleagues.

Coach's notes

There's nothing more effective than going public when it comes to tackling interruptions. If you inform colleagues that you are trying to manage your time more effectively, they may well be co-operative. It may not stop all interruptions, but it could stem the flow a bit. By explaining to colleagues what you are doing, it will avoid them thinking you are being offhand or impolite.

Whatever approaches you use to help cope with unwanted interruptions, try to be consistent and persistent. Changing your responses will give other people the impression that you can be persuaded to abandon your attempts to manage your time better. Don't allow this to happen. To recap, here are a few of the top tactics to avoid interruptions at work:

- Pre-empt interruptions by planning what actions you'll implement.
- Telephone – avoid windbags and waffling.
- Visitors – be ruthless with your time, but polite with people.
- Paperwork – don't allow yourself to be diverted by it.
- Requests and invitations – rule out anything unnecessary.
- If you're unable to say "No" – then how can anyone value your "Yes"?
- Availability – build yourself some boundaries (close door or work from home).
- Bad organization – get a strategy that you are happy with and that works for you.
- Lack of planning – without a plan you'll never make the best use of your time.

Go for it! Don't expect any of this to be easy – you may never have worked so hard in your life. Do you know what makes it difficult? You're stepping out of your comfort zone. It is always easier to carry on doing things in the same way – saying "Yes" when you really mean "No". But once you've made the effort to restrict how many interruptions you allow, you will benefit hugely.

Notes

Notes

This chapter takes a look at time management in the workplace specifically in relation to technology. Since computers dominate every aspect of life, it's not surprising that, as well as saving lots of time, they can also prove to be the biggest time wasters and stress factors of all when things go wrong – because with computers, things can go drastically wrong much more quickly. There are some common sense suggestions in this chapter for avoiding trouble, which require self-discipline and control, as well as some suggestions for saving your data.

CHAPTER 7

Technology and time management

Manage your technology

Using your machinery wisely

Most of your time at work is spent using technology of one kind or another. You may be someone who relies heavily on communicating by telephone (either a mobile or a landline) or maybe your life revolves around sending and receiving emails. Alternatively you may be paid a salary because of your ability to produce impressive, complex calculations and flow charts on computer. Whatever your work, if you want to get the most from your time, make optimum use of the technology you have available. Seemingly a lot of people either don't know how to, or simply don't want to take advantage of it. If you are busy, it makes total sense to let the machinery take the strain. To this end, anyone who wants good time management and the ability to control their stress should keep up to date with all aspects of technology – if that is humanly possible.

> **Rookie Buster**
>
> Whatever your work, if you want to get the most from your time, make optimum use of the technology you have available.

Working with computers requires confidence. You need a thorough working knowledge of the latest software packages, as well as the ability to use time-savers and short-cuts. If you have access to (but don't take advantage of) in-house training, make time to do so. This is an excellent example of what was earlier described as an important but non-urgent task. If you don't get around to learning new skills, you waste a lot of your time working inefficiently.

Making effective use of IT requires knowing what the software does. Do you use all the available features – mail-merge, templates, macros, online forms? Email was originally hailed as the start of the paperless office – but there aren't many workplaces that are free of paperwork. Emails have largely replaced memos and letters and there are many ways to avoid accumulating excess paper – start by printing only what you really need as hard copy.

If you use your IT equipment correctly it can save hours of time. Work can be produced faster and more effectively, and human resources can (and should) be used in other ways. But sometimes it is easy to forget the huge amounts of time that are wasted when things don't always go smoothly. Whether you are able to deal with problems yourself or you are required to work through the IT department, there is nothing more frustrating than sitting looking at a blank screen while urgent work waits to be done.

Some simple time saving devices which you could employ include:
- De-fragmenting the hard drive on a regular basis.
- Resisting the demands of colleagues and others to block up the computer system by downloading ephemera that fills up memory and slows operating speeds down.
- Regularly reviewing the software programs to see that you have

the most up to date versions and that your machine is compatible with those with whom you are regularly communicating.
- Familiarizing yourself with shortcuts on your PC will save hours of "click time".
- Backing up or offloading any material that isn't needed so that the hard drive is kept as free as possible. The less it contains the faster it works.
- Increasing RAM capacity if possible. This makes software programs work faster.
- Running one program at a time is often a time saver.
- Removing the majority of extraneous fonts that are provided free. This saves the temptation to tinker when producing final versions of presentation documents. Most documents are produced in the top five universally used fonts. The reason why they are universally used is because they are easily legible.
- Using scanners appropriately. They can save hours of time.
- Carrying out regular computer health-checks. Upgrade systems no more than twice a year, or when advised by your IT department – whichever is appropriate.
- Disposing of unwanted equipment and replacing it with up-to-date, cost-effective items. There are many schemes available for recycling IT equipment which include safely stripping off any old data.
- Making friends with the internet (but don't become completely attached to it). Used sensibly it can save hours of research time – but can waste a lot more if you allow yourself to be distracted on to other sites.

Being efficient where telecommunications are concerned is just as important.
- Pagers, call divert, automatic ring-back/redial, pre-programmed numbers, call-waiting and voicemail – use every kind of time saving device that your technology provides.
- Mobile phones can save hours when locations and times of meetings change at the last minute. If your work involves travelling and the train is your office annexe, keep conversation to

a minimum. How many times have you heard someone explain: "I'm on the train at the moment."

- Electronic diary software is incredibly efficient. Your system may allow you to co-ordinate meetings throughout the organization, and match available times.

There are many ways you can save time with the increasingly sophisticated technology available. These are often overlooked because you haven't had time to find out about them – but don't ignore them. Set aside some time each month (back to your time log) which you will spend learning new features to save yourself time.

Remember the mantra for communications and technology – KISS: Keep It Short and Simple.

Rookie Buster

There are many ways you can save time with the increasingly sophisticated technology available. These are often overlooked because you haven't had time to find out about them – but don't ignore them.

Backing up

There used to be two certainties in life – death and taxes. Now there are three: death, taxes and the inevitability that your computer system will go down and you'll lose all your precious data if you haven't backed it up. That will certainly propel you into a crisis where your time and stress management are concerned and possibly have far-reaching effects for your organization.

There's no doubt about it – computers are fantastic. That is, until they inexplicably stop working. When that happens, things are not quite so jolly.

(Trust me, I'm a writer, I've been there.) What you need, of course, is some form of insurance so that you can avoid disaster.

As has been mentioned, time management is related to cost. You naturally are concerned with saving time and not wasting money. But the bottom, bottom line is that you can't manage without your IT system. It doesn't matter whether your organization is minute (one person – i.e. you) or huge (almost world domination league) – no business can manage without computers. Think how much work is generated all over the globe, every day, every hour, every minute and every second on these machines. Computers enable vast amounts of work to be produced quickly, information processed at the press of a button, and presented professionally. But for some unknown reason of mechanical, electrical or alien force, all your work can suddenly disappear without a trace. Frighteningly, it is usually irrecoverable.

The professional (and personal) data on your hard drive is, without doubt, the most important and valuable thing inside your computer. Scary as this thought is, even worse is the fact that it is the only part of your computer which cannot be replaced. It may be irritating and sometimes expensive replacing a failed memory chip, or even a processor, but there is no replacing data once it is lost. This is why you must set up – at the earliest possible opportunity if you haven't already done so – a backup system.

Rookie Buster

Although it is impossible to provide absolute guaranteed protection for your hard drive, there are a number of different ways in which you can minimize the risk of losing all your important data by making regular backups of your information.

Simple hard drive failure may be the most common cause of data loss, but you can lose information stored on your computer in several other ways including through power surges, floods, lightning and equipment failure. The threat of data loss or corruption from smart internet worms and viruses has become an increasing risk too. Although it is impossible to provide absolute guaranteed protection for your hard drive, there are a number of different ways in which you can minimize the risk of losing all your important data by making regular backups of your information. Even the most secure computer can fail, causing you to lose everything you've stored electronically. One of the biggest reasons people forget about backing up is that they don't know where to start, what tools to use, or how to go about it. If you follow a few simple tips, and get into the habit of making regular backup copies of all critical information on your computer, you can protect yourself from the worst disasters.

Choose the information you want to back up. The amount of files you choose determines how much memory you need. Consider backing up any financial information, software, music and photos as well as all Word documents and your email address book.

Use the force – but which method should you choose?

There are several tools you can use to back up your computer. You can choose from an external hard drive, CD-RW, DVD-RW, tape, hard drives (internal and external), USB flash drive or online service that offers backup storage. You can also use third party back-up managers, ranging from small programs to full online backup services. Ensure you have the appropriate equipment to utilize the type of storage you choose. The different methods vary widely in price, size and ease of use. Some, like external hard drives, provide instructions for how to back up files. Selecting the right tool for the job is always best. You may need to do some research on the advantages of each, and select the one that will best suit your needs. Backup devices or tools include:

- **Recordable CDs** – CDs are inexpensive, but are slow to copy and offer limited storage capacity. They are fine for home users with little information to back up.

- **Recordable DVDs** – DVDs provide much more storage capacity than CDs, but are slower than other backup methods. Check that your computer has a DVD drive, as some older computers may not be equipped to save files this way.
- **USB flash drives** – These are sometimes called "thumb" drives because of their size. They are small, fast and easily transportable, though they tend to be expensive compared to CDs and DVDs and have relatively little storage capacity. They're perfect for moving documents from one computer to another, but not ideal for backing up large amounts of information.
- **External hard drives** – These are the most expensive, but certainly the most effective backup tool. They have huge storage capacity and allow for extremely fast copying of files. They also allow for easy overwriting of previous backups, and rapid recovery of stored information.

Prepare your backup device of choice. If you are using a hard drive, it's best to use it just for backup purposes. Make sure whatever you are using is ready to accept the backup. Open your choice of programs, select the files you wish to keep, select the media where you will be saving the backup, and start it up.

Make sure your backup process completes successfully before using your computer again.

Backing up your computer can take a long time, especially if you have quite a bit of data you would like to keep. Plan the backup for a time when your computer will be on (or when you deliberately leave it on), and at a time when you will not be using the files. Do not use a computer while a backup is in progress. If you change a file during the backup operation, you will not know which version was actually saved. Or worse still, you could halt or corrupt the backup. It will also slow your computer down.

Set a schedule to back up all of your important files. Depending on how often you use your computer and alter the files, you can set it to run however often you like. Remember to have media ready and the computer on when it is time for backups.

> **Rookie Buster**
>
> Do not use a computer while a backup is in progress. If you change a file during the backup operation, you will not know which version was actually saved. Or worse still, you could halt or corrupt the backup. It will also slow your computer down.

Make backups a regular habit. Depending on how much you use your computer (and how many new files you create in a given week), it's a good idea to set a regular time (weekly, every two weeks, or monthly) to make your backups.

If possible, store your backup device in a different place to where your computer is kept. Keep your backups in a safe place away from environmental hazards. Depending on how important the backups are, fire safes and safety deposit boxes are great places to keep backup media. If they are not so critical, filing cabinets or desks are fine too.

Keep important files in one place on your computer – perhaps a specific folder – so that it is easy to back up.

Become familiar with your computer's backup tools. Most operating systems provide backup software designed to make the process easier.

Coach's notes

The importance of technology is that it does make things happen faster, but it can also be a huge waste of time if not used correctly, or, even worse, if things go wrong. As a good time management exponent, don't allow your technology to waste your time.

- Keep up with upgrades and replace machines when appropriate (but not just because a shiny new model is on the market and you prefer the look of it).
- Become familiar with all the features of your computer and use the time saving tips and devices.
- Control yourself when surfing the internet and set time boundaries.
- Make sure you use telecommunications efficiently – auto features in particular.
- Use mobile technology – take advantage of the "anywhere" office.
- Remember to KISS: Keep It Short and Simple.

Go for it! Some people have a good working relationship with computers, while others don't. Whichever type of person you are, keep an eye on the time and stress management aspects of dealing with technology. If you love using computers, you are likely to spend far too long "playing" with new features and not working. If you don't get on with them so well and are a bit resistant to change, you may be avoiding using them correctly and taking longer to do things than you should. The point here is that alongside the benefits of using technology you must keep an eye on your time management habits.

Notes

If you are attempting to make the most of your time and keep your stress within normal limits, there are two things that continually conspire against your success. These are people and paper. If you have too much of either, your time can be eroded and you won't remain calm for long. This chapter deals with how to control paperwork and describes some tried and tested methods of keeping your desk clean and your mind clear.

CHAPTER 8

Paper: one of the greatest time wasters

Paper generally

Paperwork is something that can reduce strong people to tears. Think of the hours in life that are spent filling in forms, which then have to be processed, disseminated, stored and so on. Paper can be the bane of your life. The average person apparently spends around 175 hours a year looking for misplaced information. (This figure is probably an underestimate if you include looking for electronic paperwork too.) Efficiency and time management is directly measurable by your ability to find the right information in the quickest possible time. It is said that 60 per cent of all paperwork is disposable or irrelevant – which is bad news for all those rainforests that have been destroyed for no good reason.

If you want to control paper, you need to know the answers to the following:
1. What information is important.
2. What form it should be kept in.
3. How long it needs to be kept.
4. Who needs to know where it is.

People tend to fall into two main categories where paper is concerned. There are some who love it. They read things avidly and keep absolutely everything, whether it's relevant or useful or not. Their homes and offices resemble museums – piles and piles of old newspapers, magazines, reports, letters, postcards from colleagues, lists, used envelopes – because they are convinced that one day it might come in useful.

Other people are paper-phobic; they just don't like it – at all. They are dangerous – because either they throw it away not having read it, or they leave it untouched in unopened and ignored piles. A worst-case example of this was someone who had a box containing six months' worth of personally addressed mail which had never been touched. A new assistant started work with him and discovered the box – and it took many months to tackle the backlog.

Keeping control of paper requires the same skills that you need for managing time and controlling stress: self-discipline and organization. If you have at any point nearly collapsed under the weight of piles of paper you will know why this matters. If you don't like paper, don't ignore it. Like any other problem, it won't go away – it will just increase in size.

The 5 D method

The best and quickest method of dealing with the problem of paper is this simple:

Deal with it (it could be urgent, and overdue as well).
Determine it (a future action – don't just put it back on the pile).
Delegate it (by directing or distributing it elsewhere).
Deposit it (that is, file it in an appropriate and retrievable place).
Discard it (dump it in the bin – if it isn't valuable today, it won't be tomorrow).

> **Rookie Buster**
>
> The best and quickest method of dealing with paper is this simple: **Deal with it, Determine it, Delegate it, Deposit it, Discard it.**

Deal with it

This is the once-only rule. Pick up a piece of paper and deal with it – *now*. Not later, not tomorrow. What action needs to be taken? Take a decision and make it happen. Does this piece of paper need a signature (yours or someone else's)? Do you need to raise a cheque before it can be sent off? Does this letter require an answer? Will a quick phone call or email be sufficient? Whatever action is required – take it at once.

Determine it

Taking a decision about future action is good time management. This applies equally to people and paper. Determine where to direct this piece of paper. There are usually a few possibilities. Perhaps you should forward it on to someone else, for information or for response. If it is valuable, you should file it. If it strikes you as being irrelevant, but you're not sure, mark it for review in a week's time. When it re-appears from your pending tray to your action file, and you still can't decide, discard it.

Delegate it

The art of delegation: this is a skill which is a great asset and works equally well with people and paper. It is dealt with in more detail in regard to people further on. In relation to paperwork, if you can delegate, it will of course save you valuable time. But don't delegate an action to someone else if it's simply a task you can't or won't do yourself. Neither should you delegate it to a colleague if it's something that should be discarded. Make sure you have taken the time to think through your decision to delegate. Administrative functions are things that can often safely be delegated, such as credit control, book-keeping, bank reconciliation, completion of compliance paperwork – all usually activities that have a systematic solution.

Deposit it

Do you have a filing system? It isn't the floor space around your desk, is it? For example, if you've spotted an article in a journal or magazine that you want to read, mark the relevant page and file it in your "reading" folder, or some other retrievable place. Make sure, if you have a reading file, that you go through it every month. If it's full of papers over six months old, you're never going to find time to read them, are you? These should be deposited in the waste or recycling bin.

Discard it

If you don't need something, why keep it just in case you do. The best way to keep control of paperwork is, if it's not useful, throw it out. Use the dustbin creatively. Don't accumulate unnecessary paper. If you regularly review paperwork it shouldn't pile up, cluttering your workspace or your mind. The final word on how to tackle paper: make a choice from two options – fling it or file it.

Rookie Buster

The final word on how to tackle paper: make a choice from two options – fling it or file it.

Reading

In the last section, one of the suggestions was that you create a reading file (or should it be pile?) for pieces of paper that you need to look at. Some people, if they're feeling a bit overwhelmed by the amount of paper on their desk, consign far too much to the reading pile. In order to avoid this file from getting out of control, decide how long a time limit you'll give yourself to read the contents. One month is about right – any less, and you may not have time to get to it. Anything longer, and you may never get to it at all.

One tip for limiting the size of a reading file is to date the article twice. Record the date you receive it (or decide to put it aside for future reading) and the date by which you need to have read it. It could have relevance to a conference or meeting coming up in the next two weeks. If so, make sure you've looked at it before the meeting, not after it's happened. Don't leave the paper on your desk where it could get hidden or forgotten. A simple but effective type of reading file is a concertina file with 31 pockets – one for each day of the month. Put the article in a pocket a few days before you need to read it. Make sure you look in the file each day so you don't miss anything vital.

Another version of the Turnaround File is the "43 Rule". Designate a drawer for hanging files and label them 1 to 31. Then 1 to 12. The first section relates to the days of the current month. The second represents the rest of the months of the year. You now have somewhere to store any papers (to be read, actioned, replied to by a certain date, etc.) which will come up daily during the rest of the current month, and each month thereafter through to the end of the year. (At the beginning of each month, you remove the contents from the monthly file and distribute them in whatever date order is appropriate in the 1–31 portions.)

Filing

Is this a task you enjoy, or heartily dislike? Perhaps it is one of those category C tasks that you never quite get around to? Some people hate filing so much they have to use multiple time management tricks to get it done – for example:

- Chunking: Tackling the unpleasant task bit by bit.
- Treats: If you really hate it that much, reward yourself after you've finished.
- Ten minute rule: Can't bear the thought of filing – do it for ten minutes then stop.
- Hate method: People who really hate filing do it first thing in the morning to get it done.

Whatever method you use for filing, make it something easy. If you don't dread it too much, you're more likely to get it done.

Rookie Buster

Whatever method you use for filing, make it something easy. If you don't dread it too much, you're more likely to get it done.

Clear desking

If you know you have a tendency to hoard paperwork, a clear desk is what you should aim for. To stop unwanted piles of papers accumulating on your desk, dispense with any form of in tray. It encourages others to pass on work to you, and unless you are very disciplined, the papers will lie untouched on your desk for ages until they become hidden from view by (guess what?) even more paperwork.

Don't worry that some people say "clear desk = empty mind". In fact the reverse is true. Most people function more efficiently and effectively with a clean, well-ordered workspace. If you know people who believe that huge piles of paperwork mean that they are harder-working than their empty-desk colleagues, it is a fallacy. Piles of paper mean you can get sidetracked by something that catches your attention and deflects you from the task in hand. Clear your desk and keep it that way – only the most often used items should be visible.

> **Rookie Buster**
>
> Clear your desk and keep it that way – only the most often used items should be visible.

Before starting a complex job for which a lot of concentration is needed, make sure only the papers you are working on are accessible. This will reduce your ability to become distracted. If you aren't distracted you will feel less stressed, and the job is likely to progress more smoothly.

What about clutter? Is it something that you like? Last year's postcards from colleagues, a picture from the recent office party – do such items adorn your desk? What about all those gadgets, useful pens (that don't work) and paperclips you rarely use, drawing pins (though you don't have any pin board near you)? Ban the clutter! If you are nervous about throwing things away, designate the bottom drawer of your desk. Put all the unwanted items in it. If after a month you haven't needed to open the drawer to retrieve something invaluable, you can clear it out. You will find it a liberating experience and you won't spend time looking to see what you might find, just in case you think you'll need it.

Dealing with junk mail (paper version, not electronic) is worth a mention here. A vast amount of priority work time is wasted because you're distracted by the latest offer or bargain sale that lands on your desk. Now is not the time to look at useful books, glittering gadgets, smooth laptops and other tempting tech-toys. Time equals money, and junk mail is one of the biggest time bandits.

Another way of keeping clear of the paperwork is to block out a time to do an annual review of files or archive material. Sometimes this is called "weeding". Is there a lot of outdated material that can be discarded? (Paper records, that is – I'm not talking about deleting electronic files.) The risks incurred by throwing paperwork out (securely shredding any sensitive or confidential material, of course) are far less than the potential risk of stress from information overload. If you are not burdened by unnecessary information, you are less likely to burden others with it. The more concisely you distribute information to colleagues, the more attention they will pay to you, which is good for self-esteem and career progress.

Rookie Buster

If you are not burdened by unnecessary information, you are less likely to burden others with it. The more concisely you distribute information to colleagues, the more attention they will pay to you.

Do you carry a bag to work with you? What does it contain? If it has similar stuff to the contents of the bottom drawer of your desk, the chances are you don't even know how much clutter you are carrying around with you each day. Don't allow paper to fill every part of your life. When you open your bag on the journey home to find the book you're reading and your eye falls on some paperwork which should have been handed in to your boss that morning, your stress levels will rise – I guarantee it. Be an effective time manager and look through your rucksack or workbag on a daily basis so you don't get any nasty surprises.

Coach's notes

This whole chapter is taken up with paper. Whether you like it or loathe it, there's an awful lot of it about still. You shouldn't waste your precious time looking for something that you think you may have, but don't know exactly where it is. There is plenty of advice on what to do with paperwork and how you can deal with it. The best advice, which is simple and easy to put into practice, is the 5 D Approach:
- Deal with it.
- Determine it.
- Delegate it.
- Deposit it.
- Discard it.

If you have a lot of reading matter to get through, give it a time limit. If you haven't got around to reading it in a month, you probably never will. Filing – whatever paperwork you need to keep, organize a system which is easy for you to use and which makes retrieval as hassle free as possible. Don't let yourself or your desk get clogged up with paper. Make time to clear out your office/desk/workspace. Once you've done this you will be surprised at how much freer you will feel.

Go for it! You should be able to manage your time better if you don't have the distraction of piles of paperwork. Make attempts to increase your new time management habits to include some paper management skills. There may be infinite space on your computer hard drive to keep every email you've ever received, but if you were to keep every piece of mail that arrives in your in-tray, your desk would probably collapse under the weight. Control your paperwork so that it doesn't control you.

Notes

People can occasionally be the most awful time wasters. This sounds rather harsh, but time management, as you well know, is important, and wasting time is costly. Your boss, colleagues and staff are also important, but not at your expense. When trying to get the most out of your time, people sometimes get in the way. You need to be confident enough with your time management skills to juggle both tasks and people so that you get the best result every time. This requires self-discipline and good delegation ability, among other things which will be discussed here. In terms of effective time management and people skills, good delegation is critical to developing and improving your performance and, at its best, other people too.

CHAPTER 9

People are time consuming too

Delegation

Delegation helps to create time – something everyone would like to be able to do. Many people find themselves getting bogged down in routine operational tasks. This leaves them little or no time for the important work that they should be doing. This includes strategic tasks like long term planning and business development.

Delegation is an essential time management technique. It can be defined as giving someone else the responsibility to perform a task that is actually part of your own job. Delegation is neither easy nor straightforward. It always carries an element of risk. This is because you are assigning some work which is ultimately your responsibility.

Rookie Buster

Delegation is neither easy nor straightforward. It always carries an element of risk. This is because you are assigning some work which is ultimately your responsibility.

If you are a delegate, your delegator is handing over to you a task which he has an obligation to carry out effectively. Don't mess up – or you may not get the chance to work with him again.

The big bonus of effective delegation is that it will develop the skills of the people who work for you. People in your team will become more involved in helping achieve the organization's objectives. For the delegate, the bonus is that it could fast-track you to another level of your career, if you carry out the delegated task effectively.

Increased responsibility is an important factor in improving morale and job satisfaction. It is widely observed that people who can delegate effectively have happier and more motivated staff and experience less absenteeism and staff turnover. Wouldn't you rather have a boss who was a good delegator?

When people are looking at ways to save time, delegation is the word that often springs to their lips. Learn to delegate correctly and you'll save hours of time. This is true, but if you delegate wrongly, you may wonder why things have gone so badly. People seldom delegate effectively.

> **Rookie Buster**
>
> Learn to delegate correctly and you'll save hours of time. If you delegate wrongly, you may wonder why things have gone so badly.

Mostly what happens is that people get *told* to do a job or take something on – and that is not delegation. Very often the situation is either/or: either they get dumped with something they can't cope with, or they don't get a chance to prove their worth because delegation is not implemented effectively. More often than not, it hasn't been thought through. This results in things going wrong, breakdowns, upsets and so on. This is all very de-motivating – not only for the delegate, but also for the person who is trying to offload tasks. It is something you need to be able to do, and do well, if you are going to manage your time and keep your cool.

Whether you are the delegate or the delegator, the following description of "perfect delegation" should enable you to do it, or see that it is being done, effectively. It's not important whether you are the giver or the receiver – what's paramount is that delegation should be done properly.

> **Rookie Buster**
>
> It's not important whether you are the giver or the receiver – what's paramount is that delegation should be done properly.

How to assign or allocate work to staff

If you are desperately trying to buy yourself some time, it's common sense to look and see if there are any tasks that could, or should, be passed on to a colleague or another member of staff. Bear in mind that some tasks may be routine and repetitive, and some may not. The key to effective delegation is that the work being delegated should be balanced against the availability of people and their skills. If you are a potential delegate and some routine tasks are likely to be delegated to you, make sure you have the appropriate training to do them.

If you are planning to assign work to someone, you can retain the decision-making responsibility, should it become necessary to decide upon an alternative course of action. Delegation can, if you wish, go one step further and hand authority to make decisions to the team member. This is motivating to the delegate and is an excellent example of why delegating can be so beneficial to the delegate.

Reasons not to delegate

There are plenty of good reasons for delegating work to others when you are really overworked. However, there are also a number of reasons why people don't delegate when they should. The most frequent excuse is: "It's easier to do it myself." All that happens here is continued overload for you and loss of morale for others. The reasons for not wishing to delegate usually are:

- Failure to understand the need to delegate or not knowing how to.
- Lack of confidence in team members, and therefore not giving them the authority for decision-making.
- "Nobody else can actually help": a sign of poor leadership and failure to nurture and develop skills of less experienced staff.
- Belief that asking for help indicates a lack of ability; reluctance to show any sign of weakness.
- Failure of past attempts to delegate and refusal to try again.
- Enjoyment of a particular job which should be delegated, so holding on to it even though you know the team member would enjoy the job.
- Failure to understand the management role or how to fulfil it.
- Feeling of guilt about delegating even when the staff to whom you are delegating are not overloaded – this shows a lack of reality, as delegating is something that is required of you.
- Fear of becoming dispensable, so keeping a firm hold on every job.

These reasons for failing to delegate are all unjustifiable. Anyone who is reluctant to delegate because he feels this reduces control and places reliance on other people who may be inadequate or not up to the task, should *take* control. You cannot delegate effectively if you believe the risks of delegation outweigh the potential rewards. Of course delegating is risky, and a task may not be done well initially. But that should not mean you refuse to delegate.

> **Rookie Buster**
>
> You cannot delegate effectively if you believe the risks of delegation outweigh the potential rewards. Of course delegating is risky, and a task may not be done well initially. But that should not mean you refuse to delegate.

Delegation is a skill

If you think that one or more of the above reasons applies to your experience of delegating, or being delegated to, don't worry. Like most skills, the ability to delegate can be learned. If you can get it right, or see where others have gone wrong, you will save yourself a lot of time. When you are then in a position to delegate a task, you will know how *not* to do it. More importantly, you will free yourself to deal with those important but non-urgent tasks which usually don't get done.

Here are some tips for effective delegation:
- Plan delegation well in advance.
- Think through exactly what you want done. Define a precise aim.
- Consider the degree of guidance and support needed by the delegate.
- Pitch the briefing appropriately. Check understanding.
- Establish review dates. Check understanding.
- Establish a "buffer" period at the end, in which failings can be put right.
- Delegate "whole jobs" wherever possible, rather than bits and pieces.

- Inform others involved.
- Having delegated, stand back. Do not "hover".
- Recognize work may not be done exactly as you would have done it.
- Do not "nit-pick".
- Delegate, but do not abdicate responsibility.
- Do not delegate at the last minute: work may not be done properly, or worse, not at all.

When delegating, tasks that should be considered first are: routine tasks where progress is measurable; tasks that can be planned clearly well in advance; and tasks that one of your team has expressed genuine interest in taking on.

Rookie Buster

When delegating, tasks that should be considered first are: routine tasks where progress is measurable; tasks that can be planned clearly well in advance; and tasks that one of your team has expressed genuine interest in taking on.

Don't delegate only unpleasant tasks. Subordinates who are chosen as delegates should be offered a mix of tasks. Neither should you hold on to unpleasant tasks thinking they cannot be delegated because of their nature. It is not unfair to delegate less pleasant work if you have done it yourself – delegates should learn early on that not every task can be enjoyable.

Things that can be delegated

There are plenty of things that can, and should, be delegated. Why should you delegate? Sometimes it is purely to save time; sometimes it is obvious that others can do the job more efficiently than you can.

Perhaps you know that overload is preventing you from being effective so you must pass the work on to someone else.

The kinds of tasks that can be delegated are:
- Work which should be done by another person or in another department.
- Time-consuming tasks not entailing much decision making.
- Repetitive tasks which require decision making and could help develop a team member.

The best way forward is to set a delegation plan and timetable. It can take something like eight to twelve times longer to delegate a job effectively than to do it yourself – believe it or not, that's true. (And the amount of time needed at the outset is why a lot of people fail to delegate effectively.) But if you take the time to delegate properly in the first place you will save yourself much more time in the future.

Tasks which should not be delegated

There are of course lots of things that cannot and should not be delegated. Here's another important point about effective time management – similar to the rules about important vs. urgent, and efficiency vs. effectiveness. Now it is to do with what should, or should not, be delegated. Jobs which should *not* be delegated include:
- Seeking opportunities for the enterprise.
- Setting strategic aims and objectives.
- Creating high achievement plans for the department.
- Co-ordinating activity – knowing the task that has to be done, the abilities and needs of the staff, the resources available and mixing them to achieve optimum results.
- Communicating with staff and with senior managers and colleagues.

- The training and development of your team.

If you can free yourself to do the jobs that you alone can do, you will be managing your time well and you will be controlling your stress in what could otherwise be difficult times.

> **Rookie Buster**
>
> If you can free yourself to do the jobs that you alone can do, you will be managing your time well and you will be controlling your stress in what could otherwise be difficult times.

How to delegate effectively

Once you have identified someone that you could delegate a task to, find out if their current workload would enable them to take the job on. It is essential that objectives are clear and unambiguous. A member of staff should not be in any doubt as to what is required of them – "perhaps you could take over the running of this process from now on?" is vague and open to misinterpretation. Outcomes should be measurable – remember the SMART acronym.

Each task which has been chosen as suitable for delegation should have a specification. This should state clearly:
- The objective or intended goal of the job.
- The method you have developed to do it.
- Data requirements and where/who the information comes from.
- Any aids or equipment needed to accomplish the task.
- Definition of boundaries of responsibility.
- Principal categories of decisions that have to be made.
- Any limitations on authority where making these decisions are concerned.

If you are the delegator, coaching or training of the delegate can begin when you are ready. If you are the delegate, your delegator should keep track as he delegates the job to you and monitors the process closely at first. As things progress, you will feel more confident of the task assigned to you, and the delegator can loosen his grip to simply ensuring that the job continues to be done properly. The job should get done, but it may well be in a different way. There is nothing wrong with it being done differently, as long as the specific outcome that is required has been reached and the standard at which it was carried out was acceptable. Allow staff to perform tasks in a way that suits their personality and way of working. If you've delegated a task, allow them the freedom to interpret the manner of carrying it out.

Rookie Buster

Allow staff to perform tasks in a way that suits their personality and way of working. If you've delegated a task, allow them the freedom to interpret the manner of carrying it out.

Coach's notes

Delegation is complex, but you must try to find time to learn the skill of effective delegation. Once you have achieved that you will be able to save yourself huge amounts of time in the future. One of the most important things to remember is that the delegate should be encouraged to take ownership of the task. If you are delegating, do not hover over the delegate. Should the team member encounter problems, you may need to suggest possible solutions and leave it to the delegate to choose which he prefers. If you take control of choosing the solution, you have taken back responsibility for the task, thereby removing the responsibility from the delegate back to yourself. This would be extremely demotivating for anyone and they would be unwilling and reluctant to put themselves forward for taking on new responsibilities in future.

Try to agree in advance what resources are likely to be needed; also, as an effective delegator you must sell the benefit of doing the task to the delegate and leave them room to show initiative in how they carry out the job.

Don't forget the feedback. This is a major factor in successful delegation and should be given from time to time while the work is carried out. Effective feedback should enable the delegate to improve their performance and keep their problems and concerns in perspective. Constructive feedback should be as specific as possible, but always make your remarks as objective as you can. Most people are prepared to take on responsibility in exchange for recognition. Thanking people for their efforts is most important and should if possible be done in public too, for example at departmental meetings.

Go for it! Delegation is often considered a one-way ticket, being helpful only to the person in charge. But it has a bonus effect: it is of considerable benefit to the member of staff. Whether or not you are in a position where delegation would be appropriate and possible, it is still worth knowing how to do it. It is certainly sensible to know the difference between effective delegation and bad delegation. Should you be the person who is chosen for a task, this is a huge boost to your potential development – both practically and psychologically.

Notes

Notes

In this final chapter you will learn a few more techniques for controlling stress, which in turn will help you to increase your personal effectiveness. There are also some helpful hints about how to keep up the good habits you've learned in the preceding pages.

CHAPTER 10

Motivation for keeping up the good work

Kill stress before it kills you

Many office workers suffer from unacceptable levels of stress. The reasons given are mixed but the top four are:
- Broken computers.
- Too much work.
- Demanding customers.
- Annoying colleagues.

You may currently be trying to cope with one or more of these issues. You may also be working flat out because you're trying to implement your newly acquired time management skills. You're keen to impress your boss or colleagues that you're good at your job. If you've been working long hours, your stress levels have probably risen. A result of your being stressed is that you work less effectively.

If you're working for someone else, you may sometimes spend your time doing pointless things. If you don't understand why you're doing something and it doesn't seem relevant or purposeful, you are likely to get stressed. So here's the double whammy – your stress levels increase because you're spending hours and hours working at futile things that other people want you to do. However hard you work it doesn't seem to make any difference. Because your work doesn't achieve anything, you feel demoralized and leave work stressed out. Why? Because what you've been doing all day hasn't made any improvement. The result? You wonder why you bothered. What better example of a downward spiral can there be?

Still feeling stressed you stagger into work the next day. You are trapped in your office between the hours of 9am and 5pm because that is the agreed time you go to work. During these hours you and your colleagues shuffle papers, generate unnecessary information and communicate unimportant and irrelevant things to each other by means of interminable and tedious meetings or lengthy telephone calls and emails. Some (bad) employers work hard to create activities so that people's work time is filled to capacity. Everyone knows time passes quicker if you're busy. Meanwhile, your blood pressure is rising and you're beginning to feel ill.

Rookie Buster

When it comes to stress management the key is to do something in the shortest amount of time possible and achieve a result.

Before going any further, let's make some things perfectly clear:
1. When it comes to stress management – or perhaps stress elimination is the better description here – the key is to do something in the shortest amount of time possible and achieve a result.

2. If you have eight hours to fill during the working day, you will find things to do to fill those eight hours. But if you had fifteen hours to fill, you'd fill fifteen. Conversely, if there was an emergency and you needed to leave the office in two hours but had work to finish, somehow you'd manage to complete that work in two hours flat, or effectively delegate some of it elsewhere. How does this happen?
3. Do you remember Parkinson's Law? It sort of goes hand in hand – conversely – with the Pareto Principle (or the 80/20 Rule). The difference is that Parkinson's Law dictates that a task will swell in perceived importance and complexity in relation to the time available for its completion. Does that tell you something?
4. So the magic formula for stress busting is – *the imminent deadline*. Simple, isn't it?
5. You have 24 hours to produce a detailed report and examination of the organization's performance over the last 12 months. The boss is having a meeting with the shareholders and he needs it on his desk tomorrow at 7pm. Will you manage it? Yes, because you will be focusing on achieving the result.
6. The beauty of the short deadline is that you can only do the bare essentials. No time to waste on inconsequential things. If you had ten days to complete the task, think of the size of the mountain you could create out of this molehill. What if you had two months in which to do it? Don't even go there …
7. The bonus here is that invariably the end product of the shorter deadline is of equal or higher quality due to the greater focus on the result.
8. You achieve something of tangible benefit in a short amount of time. This permits only minimal stress build-up, because of the relatively quick timescale. It is possible to be uncomfortable for a short amount of time because you know it will be over soon. If you don't know how long an unpleasant situation is going to last, it quickly becomes unbearable and stressful.
9. By the time you've got the piece of work completed, you're probably tired out. The adrenalin rush you

experienced (*healthy stress*) to accomplish the task may be wearing off. You feel exhausted, but hey, what's this? The endorphins (hormones which give you a feeling of pleasure after exertion) are kicking in because you've satisfactorily achieved the required task within the time limits and the work is to a high standard.

10. Did you notice anything missing? That's right – no *dis*tress (that is, unhealthy stress).

Another way of looking at time and stress management

Sometimes it's not enough knowing what the most important things are that you have to do. If you don't impose strict deadlines that create focus you'll never achieve them. Don't spend any more time getting stressed, jumping from one interruption and futile task to another. Start eliminating stress before it eliminates you, and you'll find you've also cracked the problem of time management.

> **Rookie Buster**
> Sometimes it's not enough knowing what the most important things are that you have to do. If you don't impose strict deadlines that create focus you'll never achieve them.

If you can manage it, a clever and useful method of controlling stress and working effectively is to *combine* the Pareto Principle (or 80/20 Rule – the one that states that 80 per cent is often good enough, and that 20 per cent of effort produces 80 per cent of results) with Parkinson's Law (which teaches us to shorten work time on tasks in order to keep their importance in proportion). Identify a few critical tasks that contribute most towards getting job satisfaction and schedule them with very short, clear deadlines. What you now have is effective time management with minimal stress.

Being flexible is important too

Now that you are (almost!) an expert at time and stress management, let's have a look at your flexibility levels. Change happens and there's not much you can do about it. Some people ignore it, others try to stop it. You could try insulating yourself from it, while others spend an enormous amount of energy fighting it. If you are going to work effectively and eliminate unhealthy stress from your life, having the ability to adapt to change easily will positively enhance your career prospects and give your self-esteem a boost.

> **Rookie Buster**
>
> If you are going to work effectively and eliminate unhealthy stress from your life, having the ability to adapt to change easily will positively enhance your career prospects and give your self-esteem a boost.

There are usually four phases through which people pass before they embrace change. These are:

1. **Denial**
   "That's never going to work." "We tried that already." Do you recognize the ostriches in your organization? They may have their heads in the sand, but change is not going to go away as a result of their not seeing it.

2. **Resistance**
Some people try to stick with the old ways of doing things: "But it's always worked OK in the past." The reality is, the sooner you get to grips with the new system, the better it is for your career (and your blood pressure).

3. **Exploration**
Maybe the change doesn't have to be all bad. Is it possible that there are some advantages to a new way of working? If you look at the change with a more open mind, you may begin to find there are some good things that come from it.

4. **Acceptance**
Once you reach this stage, you may even find that the new system works better than you'd believed possible. You have by this time fully integrated the change into your own routine.

Don't be a blocker

If you have serious doubts about a new method of working which has been introduced, there are ways of dealing tactfully with this. Let's say your boss arrives one morning full of excitement and explains that in future a job is going to be done in a particular way. If your first response is, "Oh, what a ridiculous idea: that'll never work," don't be surprised if he or she retaliates aggressively.

You are of course entitled to your opinion, but there are better ways of expressing your doubts. You could for example respond by saying, "Well, that idea has its merits, but it may not get us the result we need." Although still disagreeing, you are not going head to head in a confrontation. Your boss can accept your comments without any reason to raise the temperature, and the discussion can continue. The meaning behind your words may still be "I don't buy it," but your behaviour (that is, the way the remark is delivered) is entirely different. And if your boss respects your viewpoint, he or she may well respond along the lines of "OK then, it was just a suggestion. What would you propose?"

You need to look out for blocking behaviour and avoid it if you are going to continue the good work with your newly acquired time management and stress control skills. You must not allow yourself to resist change (unless you have a valid point to make). Neither must you permit others who are resistant to change to affect your ability to work productively. There are bound to be people who will try, and they could impede your progress. If their attitude is entrenched, your personal effectiveness and productivity as well as your stress levels will be adversely affected.

> **Rookie Buster**
>
> You must not allow yourself to resist change (unless you have a valid point to make). Neither must you permit others who are resistant to change to affect your ability to work productively.

Watch out for the warning signs: these are some of the things people may do if they cannot accept change:

- Use old methods of working when they should be playing by the new rules.
- Avoid taking on new assignments for fear that they might have to work in a different way.
- Try to slow things down to their own pace. Change usually requires people to speed up, so they risk getting left further and further behind.
- Play the victim/martyr role (but more flexible colleagues are unlikely to show them any sympathy).
- Try to control the uncontrollable. This is a bit like attempting to stop the tide from coming on to the beach. Change is inevitable – they'll have to accept it. Instead of wasting energy resisting it, they need to learn to go with the flow.

You may be able to identify some of your colleagues whose behaviour is similar to that described above. Don't be swept along with them. If you can instead show your employers that you are willing to embrace change, they will quickly realize what an incredible asset you are to the organization. Your positive attitude and your ability to react and be flexible to new ways of doing things will indicate you're a survivor. Your responsiveness to change will be your passport to future success.

Rookie Buster

If you can show your employers that you are willing to embrace change, they will quickly realize what an incredible asset you are to the organization.

Coach's notes

You are familiar with the expression "No pain, no gain." There's a similar saying for the workplace: "No stress, no success." Stress is an essential ingredient to achieving your goals if you are ambitious. When it comes to reconciling stress with your time management, both must be kept in proportion. Someone who has no stress is unlikely to be a high achiever and therefore won't be worrying unduly about his or her time management skills. On the other hand there is no point in being a high achiever if you don't live long enough to enjoy your success!

Getting the balance right is the solution. If you are able to exercise a degree of flexibility at work, it will go a long way to keeping stress levels within acceptable limits. This applies not only to processes but also to your thinking. If you think in the right way, you are better able to carry out tasks effectively. Remember the difference between reactive and proactive working? Think well and you'll do well.

If you can think "out of the box" you may come up with some innovative methods for doing things. Being creative helps you to remain positive. Being positive stops you from suffering from "overwhelm". If you're not overwhelmed, you must be managing your time well. Good time managers don't suffer from excessive stress. And so it goes on – it's a virtuous circle.

Go for it! When you are trying to stay calm, you need to control as much of your working life as possible. This is sometimes difficult when tough situations occur. On the whole, optimists cope better than pessimists, and they get better results from those around them, too: half full glasses are always more attractive than half empty ones.

If the going is tough, remain as focused as you can. Concentrating on one particular aspect of the task should make things easier. Rewards are necessary and helpful, and celebrating successes (even if they are small ones) does wonders for your self-esteem.

Notes

You may at times find it difficult to keep a positive outlook when you're not only working hard to achieve more of the right things (by doing fewer of the wrong things), but at the same time also keeping your stress at a healthy level. There is a lot of effort involved and there's plenty of stuff for you to think about. Let's be clear about one thing – a lot of what you achieve is down to your attitude. Here is a brief re-cap.

APPENDIX
Attitude training

Negative situations and attitudes

Problems occur here ...

- If you can't work out your priorities, you'll never manage your time.
- You must control interruptions – whether by phone, email or people.
- Overcome your habit of procrastinating: don't delay – do it now.
- Crises must be dealt with fast. Today's emergency is tomorrow's disaster.

"Overwhelm" is when you:

- Regularly spend more than 10 hours a day working.
- Have to take work home three or more times a week.
- Suffer sleepless nights and/or dream about your job.
- Have recently been forced by pressure of work to cancel social plans.

Stress is:

- A mismatch between perceived demands and perceived ability to cope.
- Not being able to work out how important things really are, compared with how important they seem to you. If you couldn't finish your work, would it really matter? Could someone else cover for you?
- Something you need to reduce, otherwise you will find it more difficult to manage your time.

Office "time bandits"

- Disorganization: untidy desks – unworkable systems.
- Interruptions: unexpected calls, tasks, visitors.
- Meetings: unnecessary attendance at conferences, seminars, workshops.
- Paperwork: deal with it at once; decide if it is urgent, important or irrelevant.

Positive attitudes and solutions

Resolutions

- Golden rule: nothing gets easier if it's left – the reverse is true.
- Use your personal strengths: they are often ignored or undervalued.
- Be realistic, not perfect: no one can (or should) do everything.
- Big project? Try tackling it in a different way.
- Create a buffer zone: find or make an interruption-free area.

Procrasti-killers

- Salami technique: break a big task into small, thin slices.
- 5-minute plan: anyone can do anything (however unpleasant) for five minutes.
- Do the worst first: get the nastiest job out of the way early on.
- Reward yourself: follow an unpleasant task with one you enjoy.
- Go public: tell someone your deadline – commit yourself.

Good habits

- Make a note: if you write it down, you shouldn't forget it.
- Chunking: block out space in your schedule or diary to focus on priorities.
- Delay reaction: reflect rather than react to situations.
- Delegate: don't muddle through – enlist help or distribute work.
- Targets: achievable goals and clearly defined objectives are best.

SMART working

- **S**PECIFIC: know what you want to achieve.
- **ME**ASURABLE: know how much use it will be.
- **A**CHIEVABLE: make sure you can actually do it.
- **R**ELEVANT: does it really matter?
- **T**IME BASED: how long is it going to take?

The Pareto Principle (the 80/20 Rule)

- 20 per cent of your day is spent on important tasks.
- 80 per cent of your working day just gets used up.
- So – limit tasks to the important in order to shorten work time.

Parkinson's Law

- A task will swell in perceived importance and complexity in relation to the time available for its completion.
- So – shorten work time to keep the importance of tasks in proportion.

This is a delightfully curious phenomenon: two different approaches for increasing effective time management and reducing stress which are inversions of the other. Think about it. For best results – use both together. Identify the few critical tasks that contribute most to your personal effectiveness and schedule them with *very short* and *clear* deadlines.

Don't allow yourself to indulge in any negative statements, such as "I'll never be able to do all this; how can I remember everything?" Instead, be positive and tell yourself, "This is going to help me manage my time and save me loads of stress." Remember that all you've read in the preceding pages has been tried and tested and *actually works*. People can really save time and stress by following this advice and these suggestions.

If you're going through a difficult patch:
- Train your brain to accept only the messages you want to accept.
- Don't allow it to absorb negative information.
- When faced with a problem, look for a solution – not a reason to give up.
- If something you try to do doesn't work, don't be afraid to try again later …
- … or if you prefer, try something different.
- Remember, you only fail when you quit!

Finally, in the words of Henry Ford, "Whether you think you can, or whether you think you can't – either way, you're right."

Index

4 D Approach 64–5
5 D method of dealing with paperwork 82, 114–16, 121
5-minute plan 153
43 Rule 117
80/20 Rule (Pareto Principle) 20, 40, 52, 82, 141, 142–3, 153

absences from work, as a result of stress 33, 34, 37–8, 40
acceptance of change 143, 144
anxiety 33
assigning work to staff 127–8
attitudes 150
    negative 151–2, 154
    positive 152–4

backing up 103, 104–8
backup software 108
backups
    scheduling 107, 108
    storage of 108
bags 120
balancing activities (work/life balance) 28, 39
Belbin team roles 46–9

blocking behaviour 144–5
blue-sky thinking 74–5
body, looking after 39, 40
bottom line, time management and 20–1
brainstorming 74–5
breaks 39
buffer zones 95, 152
bullying 35, 38
bundling
    of interruptions 87
    of tasks 66, 69
burnout (overwhelm) 29, 33, 147, 151
"busyness", confused with "output" 18, 72

CD-RW 106, 107
change 40, 143–6
    inability to respond to 21, 26
    resistance to 17, 143–4, 144–6
changes, making 52–4
chaos, overcoming 12, 19
chats 93–4
chunking 64, 67, 69, 79, 118, 153
clear desking 118–20, 121
closed door rule 93, 96

clutter 119
Co-ordinators 48
colleagues
    perceptions of you 12
    as sources of interruptions 86, 88–9, 93–4
    as time wasters 93–4, 124
common sense 39, 40
communication 8, 21
Completer-Finishers 48, 49
computers 100, 100–4, 109, 110
    backing up 103, 104–8
conferences 94–5, 152
confidential material 120
control
    feeling a lack of 14, 31, 32, 74
    taking control 38, 39, 52–4, 55, 61, 93, 128, 134, 147
corruption of data 106
costs of poor time management 20–1
creativity 18, 29, 55, 147
    in planning 78
crises 18, 20, 23, 74, 86, 151
crisis management 20, 60–1, 78, 81, 87

daily plans 80
data loss 104–6
deadlines 45–6, 61, 65, 79
    for goals 75
    imminent 141–2, 142–3, 154
    short and clear 154
    short-term 67
Deal with it 114, 115
decision making 14, 20
    authority for 127–8
decluttering 119, 121
delaying reaction 64, 82, 153
delaying tactics *see* procrastination
Delegate it 114, 115–16
delegation 15, 17, 50, 51, 79, 124, 125–7, 134–5, 153
    assigning work to staff 127–8
    effective 124, 129–30, 132–3, 134, 135
    inability to delegate 17, 128–9
    of paperwork 115–16
    suitable tasks 65, 130–1
    unsuitable tasks 131–2
denial of change 143
Deposit it 114, 116
depression 29, 33, 34
    "digital depression" 32
desks, clear 118–20, 121
Determine it 114, 115
diaries, electronic 104
diary decisions 64
"digital Darwinism" 32
"digital depression" 32
Discard it 114, 116
disorganization 152
distractions 51, 52, 55
"Do your best and leave the rest" 38
doing things one at a time 23, 80, 82
DVD-RW 106, 107

effectiveness 11, 12–13, 16, 58, 63, 76, 87, 88
efficiency 12, 16, 76
    information and 113
effort to time ratio 80–1, 83
electronic diaries 104
elimination 91
emails 8, 51, 69, 87, 93, 95, 102
exercise 40
exhaustion 28, 29
exploration of change 144
external hard drives 106, 107

fear
    of becoming dispensable 128
    of failure 19
    of tasks 70
    of the unknown 17
feedback, in delegation 134

Index

"fight" or "flight" mode 32
files, weeding 120
filing 116, 118, 121
    reading file 116, 117
fire fighting 8, 23
    see also crises; crisis management
fire safes 108
flash drives 106, 107
flexibility 17, 19, 143–6, 147
flexible working 53–4, 92
fling it or file it 116
Ford, Henry (1863–1947) 154

gatekeepers 89
goals 153
    definition 75–6
    setting 16
    short-term 79–80
going public 67–8, 77, 96
"good enough" 20, 82, 142

hard drives 105–6, 106, 107
hate method for filing 118
health issues 29, 35–6, 37–8, 39, 40
Health and Safety Executive, UK (HSE), definition of stress 33
heart disease, stress and 34
Hooke, Robert (1635–1703), concept of stress 27–8
HSE (Health and Safety Executive, UK), definition of stress 33

"iceberg syndrome" 34, 35
immune system, stress and 34
Implementers 48
importance of tasks 58, 59–63, 70
in trays 118
inability to delegate 17, 128–9
inability to plan 19
inability to respond to change 21, 26
inability to say "No" 23, 96
individual stress 35–7

information 113, 120
instant gratification 8
internet 103, 109
interruptions 19, 23, 51, 52, 86, 97, 151, 152
    classifying 89–90
    managing 86, 90–5, 96
    people as causes of 86, 88–9, 93–4
    saying "No" to 87–9, 91, 96
invitations 94–5, 96
irritability 29, 34
IT *see* computers

job satisfaction 126, 142
junk mail 119
"just do it" 64, 65

KISS (Keep It Short and Simple) 104, 109

lack of time 11–12, 18
"late taskers" 45–6
long hours 23, 31, 139, 151
looking after yourself 39, 40
loss of control 21
lost opportunities 21
low morale 21, 128

maintenance tasks 78–9
making changes 52–4
making notes 153
medium term plans 79
meetings 94–5, 151
message taking 92
mistakes 8, 21, 38
mobile technology 103–4, 109
Monitor-Evaluators 48
morale 126
    low 21, 128
motivation 128, 134
    lack of 21

natural energy 44, 45–6, 55, 63
negative attitudes 151–2, 154
negative situations 151–2
negative stress 13, 28, 29, 30, 32–4, 37–8, 39
    symptoms 28, 33–4, 37
networking 94–5
"No", saying 23, 82, 87–9, 91, 96
"No stress, no success" 147
notes, making 153

objectives 76–7, 153
    for delegates 132
    planning 78, 79
"on call", being 8
once-only rule for dealing with paperwork 115
online backup services 106
operational tasks 51
opportunities, lost 21
optimists 148
organizational procedures 20
organizational stress 34, 34–5, 35–6
organized approach 14, 23, 24, 82, 96
"output", "busyness" confused with 18, 72
outsourcing 65
over-scheduling 80
overload 33, 128
overwhelm 29, 33, 147, 151

panics 18
paperwork 96, 102, 112, 113–14, 122, 152
    5 D method of dealing with 82, 114–16, 121
    clear desking 118–19, 121
    once-only rule 115
    see also filing; reading
Pareto Principle (80/20 Rule) 20, 40, 52, 82, 141, 142–3, 153
Parkinson's Law 52, 141, 142–3, 154

people 112
    as sources of interruptions 86, 88–9, 93–4
    as time wasters 93–4, 124
perfection 20, 38, 53, 152
personal reserve 39
personal strengths 45–6, 55, 56, 152
personal style 42, 43–4, 45–6, 55, 63
    self-assessment 44–5, 46–9
personality types 48–9
pessimists 148
phone 8, 69, 90, 92, 95, 96, 103–4
planning 12, 13, 14–15, 18, 23, 78–80, 96, 125
    done the night before 68
    inability to plan 19
    making a plan 15, 18–19
    time-specific 78
plans 79–80
    strategic 79, 125
Plants 48
positive attitudes 152–4
positive solutions 152–4
positive stress 28, 29, 30, 32, 33, 39, 40
priorities 12, 16, 51, 52, 60–1, 63, 151, 153
prioritizing 58–63, 65, 69, 70, 77–8, 82, 91
    4 D Approach 64–5, 82
proactive approach 73, 74, 79–80, 81, 82, 83, 147
    techniques 74–8
process tasks 51
procrastination 19–20, 23, 69, 70
    4 D Approach 64–5, 82
    overcoming 64–8, 82, 151, 153
productivity 13, 40, 87
    delegation and 17
    demands for increased 8, 32
progress tasks 78–9

raising awareness of stress 36

reactive approach 73–4, 76, 81, 82, 83, 147
reading 117, 121
reading file 116, 117
recordable CDs 106, 107
recordable DVDs 106, 107
reducing stress, benefits of 34
relaxation 40
rescheduling tasks 80
resistance to change 17, 143–4, 144–6
Resource Investigators 48
resources, waste of 21
responsibility 126, 134
rewards 69, 118, 148
routine tasks 51, 55, 62, 125, 127, 130
ruts, getting stuck in 17

safety deposit boxes 108
salami technique 153
　see also chunking
saying "No" 23, 82, 91
　to interruptions 87–9, 91, 96
scheduling backups 107, 108
self management 13
self-analysis of stress levels 30–1
self-assessment 15, 44–5, 46–9
setting goals 16
Shapers 48
short-term plans 79–80
short-term targets 67
sickness absence, because of stress 33, 34, 37–8, 40
SMART principle 75, 76, 78, 132, 153
social chats 93–4
software 102, 102–3
　backup software 108
sources of stress 32–3
spam 93
Specialists 48
staff absences, because of stress 33, 34, 37–8, 40
starting the day 14–15, 118

strategic plans 79, 125
stress 24, 26, 27–30, 32, 152
　benefits of reducing 34
　as a cost of poor time management 21
　individual 35–7
　levels of different tasks 62–3
　management of 8–9, 28, 29, 30, 38–40, 110, 140–2
　negative 13, 28, 29, 30, 32–4, 37–8, 39
　organizational 34, 34–5, 35–6
　positive 28, 29, 30, 32, 33, 39, 40
　raising awareness of 36
　self-analysis 30–1
　sources of 32–3
　staff absences because of 33, 34, 37–8, 40
　symptoms 28, 29, 33–4, 37
　underlying causes 37–8
　in the workplace 32–7, 139–40
stress diaries 30, 31
stress limits, individual 27, 30
stress management 8–9, 28, 29, 30, 38–40, 110, 140–2
success 146, 147, 148
surprise, elements of 23
SWOT (Strengths, Weaknesses, Opportunities and Threats) analyses 75
symptoms of stress 28, 29, 33–4, 37

taking control 38, 39, 52–4, 55, 61, 93, 128, 134, 147
tapes, for backup 106
targets 153
　short-term 67
tasks 23
　bundling 66, 69
　categorizing 62–3, 69
　importance 58, 59–63, 70
　maintenance tasks 78–9

progress tasks 78–9
rescheduling 80
routine tasks 51, 55, 62, 125, 127, 130
unpleasant 55, 66, 67, 118, 130, 153
urgency 8, 59–63, 70, 91
team roles (Belbin) 46–9
Team Workers 48
technology 8, 100
and stress 32, 110
and time management 105, 109, 110
see also computers
telecommunications 103–4, 109
telephone 8, 69, 90, 92, 95, 96, 103–4
ten minute rule 118
thanking people 134
thinking 8, 17
outside the box 17, 147
"thumb" drives 106, 107
time 11
lack of 11–12, 18
"time bandits" 152
time logs 44, 49–52, 59–60, 89–90
time management 7–9, 10, 11–12, 13, 16
benefits of 12–13, 21, 40
to combat negative stress 30
costs of poor time management 20–1
and technology 105, 109, 110
time saving devices, when using IT 102–3
time specific plans 78

time wasters 51, 52
time wasters (people) 93–4, 124
To Do lists 14–15, 55, 69
treats 118
see also rewards
Turnaround File 117

underachievement 21
unpleasant tasks 55, 66, 67, 118, 130, 153
urgency of tasks 8, 59–63, 70, 91
Urgency/Importance grid 59–63
USB flash drives 106, 107

viruses 106
visitors 96, 152
voicemail 82, 90, 103

weeding of files 120
work environment 38
work/life balance 28, 39
workbags 120
working day, scheduling tasks during 62–3
working from home 53–4, 92, 96
working harder, not the solution 23, 31, 36–7, 83, 140
working smarter 23, 83
workplace absences, because of stress 33, 34, 37–8, 40
workplace stress 32–7, 139–40
workplace stress MOT 36
worms 106